THE LIFE OF GEORGE GERSHWIN

PHOTOGRAPH BY EDWARD STEICHEN

THE LIFE OF

George Gershwin

ROBERT RUSHMORE

THE CROWELL-COLLIER PRESS, New York

COLLIER-MACMILLAN LTD., London

Grateful acknowledgment is made to the following:
New World Music Corporation for permission to quote "Swanee," © MCMXIX, Copyright Renewed; "Somebody Loves Me," © MCMXXVI, Copyright Renewed; "Fascinating Rhythm," © MCMXXIV, Copyright Renewed; "Man I Love," © MCMXXIV; "Someone to Watch Over Me," © MCMXXVI, Copyright Renewed; "Do-Do-Do," © MCMXXVI, Copyright Renewed; " 'S Wonderful," © MCMXXVII, Copyright Renewed; "I'm A Typical Self-Made American," © MCMXXX, Copyright Renewed; "Finaletto Scenè IV-Act I," © MCMXXXII, Copyright Renewed; "Embraceable You," © MCMXXX, Copyright Renewed.

Library of Congress Catalog Card Number: AC-66-10312

FIRST PRINTING

The Macmillan Company, New York
Collier-Macmillan Canada Ltd, Toronto, Ontario
Printed in the United States of America

For

JAY HAMBURGER

and

ALLEN SHAWN

and all the other

young Gershwin fans

Contents

"Jazz is music; it uses the same notes as Bach used. . . . It is an original American achievement that will endure, not as jazz perhaps, but which will leave its mark on future music in one way or another."

George Gershwin

The bustling streets of New York's Lower East Side, where George Gershwin grew up. CULVER PICTURES, INC.

1 / Fascinating Rhythm

SCHOOL WAS OUT and the boy had gone roller-skating—his favorite pastime. Restless, energetic, hating school, he loved the excitement of roller skating, the feeling it gave him of getting somewhere fast. It also happened to be the best way of traveling around New York City. Dodging in and out among ladies with long full skirts and enormous hats, trying to beat out a horse-drawn wagon or, better still, one of the new horseless carriages, he could make it to Harlem and back home to his Lower East Side neighborhood easily in a morning.

That afternoon, however, he had decided to stay near home, scouting the neighborhood for friends or maybe a not-so-friendly street fight. Pausing for a breather at an intersection, he scanned both avenues carefully with his dark, intent eyes. To a passerby young George Gershwin—for that was the boy's name—might have looked just like any ordinary tough city kid with a dirty face and an impudent smile. But a few might have noticed that behind the brashness of his expression lay a strange sensitivity which didn't seem to go with the rest of his appearance.

Suddenly George stiffened. Far down the street he had seen a small figure hurrying along, staying close to the buildings to keep from sight an object that he was carrying in his hand. With an exclamation of delight George started skating toward the figure. He was a boy from George's school, and George had recognized the object in the boy's hand—a violin. Hurtling down on him, George began shouting, "Maggie! Maggie!" The boy started to run. Other kids playing in the street took up the cry. "Maggie! Maggie!" Pursued by the jeering name, the boy rounded the corner, dashed up a flight of steps and disappeared through a door to safety.

What a curse to have to take music lessons and be called a Maggie, thought George as he skated away, though the funny thing was that he rather liked music. Songs like "Annie Laurie" and "Old Black Joe" that they sang in school were really kind of nice, and once, when he was about six, he could remember standing outside a penny arcade, absolutely rooted by the funny jumps in a piece of music called "The Melody in F" coming from a player piano. Sometimes, too, when he skated up to Harlem he would hang around a nightclub where a bunch of colored musicians were rehearsing a curious kind of music with jerky rhythms which he also found fascinating.

The truth was that whenever he heard music he liked it very much, but what he heard didn't really amount to anything. The new invention, the phonograph, was still a toy of the very rich, and the records sounded pretty squawky anyway. The radio, of course, had not been invented at all. Most of the music that George heard was the popular songs people sang or played in their own homes—like "Take Me Out to the Ball Game" or "Down by the Old Mill Stream." But in the Gershwin house nobody played or sang at all, except when Mr. Gershwin, who liked to clown, would render a selection on a piece of tissue paper and a comb. That was the only musical instrument in the house. And maybe it was just as well, George thought, because if the Gershwins got a piano like some of their friends and neighbors (often because it was supposed to be a classy thing to own) then he might have to take lessons and endure the torments of being called a Maggie, too.

George had a baby sister, Frances, and when she was a little bit older it would be safe for them to own a piano because it was considered all right for girls to take lessons. Just not boys. Boys—so went the thinking—should be out playing games or *doing* things. That was the American tradition. Men by *doing* things had created a great new country. They weren't like European men with their fancy ways and interest in idle things like art and music. If music fitted into a man's life in America, like a song that helped pass the time when he worked or a hymn on Sunday or a good tune to dance and relax to, that was all right. But not the other kind of music that you just sit and listen to, with strange titles like "Rhapsody" or "Prelude" or "Concerto" which don't mean anything and composers with unpronounceable foreign names like Beethoven or Rimski-Korsakov or Tchaikovsky.

True, George Gershwin's parents were foreigners. They had come to New York City from Russia in the 1890's to escape the oppressions of Czarist rule and find a better life. Mr. and Mrs. Gershwin often addressed each other in their native tongue, and the way they used English was more colorful than accurate. But the children—Ira, born December 6, 1896, George, born September 26, 1898, Arthur and Frances—were Americans, with American ways and attitudes and a feeling for American traditions—one of which was teasing boys who took music lessons.

So George Gershwin might have continued like any other average city kid, getting bad marks at school, fighting in the streets and making fun of the Maggies, if his whole life

A family outing in Prospect Park. George is seated in the middle, between the maid and his mother, with Arthur on the left and Ira on the right.

CULVER PICTURES, INC.

hadn't been changed by a boy at school two years younger than he was. And this boy was, of all things, one of the Maggies that George so despised.

His name was Max Rosenzweig (later shortened to Rosen) and at eight years old he was already a violin virtuoso, a child prodigy. One day it was announced that little Max Rosenzweig would play at a school entertainment to be held after the lunch recess. Since attendance was voluntary, George Gershwin unhesitatingly chose to get into a ball game going on in the school yard over hearing some kid scratch away on a violin. The concert began. From the assembly room an open window gave onto the yard. In the middle of the ball game George suddenly stopped playing, transfixed by the strains of Dvořák's famous *Humoresque* being played on the violin. Never, it seemed, had he heard anything like it. The music was "like a flashing revelation of beauty," he said later of the experience.

All scorn for boys who took music lessons completely forgotten, George waited outside the school door hoping to make friends with Rosenzweig when he came out. It began to rain but George doggedly stood in the doorway for an hour and a half. Finally, soaked to the skin, he went inside the school and discovered that Rosenzweig had left by the teachers' entrance.

Undaunted, Gershwin found out where the boy violinist lived and presented himself in a dripping state on the doorstep, only to discover that he had missed him again. But the Rosenzweig family was so amused by the excitement of their son's unknown admirer that they arranged for George to come back and meet him. "From the first moment we became the closest of friends," Gershwin reminisced in later years. "We chummed about arm in arm; we lavished childish affection upon one another; . . . we exchanged letters even when only a weekend and some hundred blocks lay between us. Max opened the world of music to me. When we'd play hooky together, we'd talk eternally about music—that is, when we weren't wrestling. I used to throw him every time, by the way, though he was one of those chubby, stocky kids."

Having had an excellent musical education, Max was able to tell his new friend stories of the lives of the great composers and to try to describe the music that they had written. Growing more and more interested and excited, George next began to think of making music himself, perhaps by experimenting on a piano. There wasn't one in his own home. The only thing to do was to ask if he could use one in the house of a friend. With permission obtained, for the first time in his life George Gershwin sat down at a keyboard and tried to pick out the tunes that he knew from school, such as "Annie Laurie" and "Old Black Joe" with his right hand, while filling in some kind of harmony with his left.

Stop and think for a moment of the difficulties that faced him. Picking out a melody with one finger on the piano was no problem for anyone with the quick, receptive ear that Gershwin had even at the age of ten. But what about the harmony? Harmony, after all, is like grammar in a language. To make a sentence there are a variety of words to choose from and many different ways in which to arrange them. Still, they must follow one another in a certain basic sequence to convey meaning.

So too with harmony. There are numbers of different chords that can be used to harmonize the melody of a song like "Annie Laurie"; nonetheless, certain chords must follow others for the language of music to sound meaningful to our ears. Gershwin knew nothing of the rules of harmony nor had he heard enough music to be able to imitate correct harmonic progressions. All he could do was experiment, finding out which chord seemed to fit best within the pattern of the melody and which chords followed each other most satisfyingly. Persistence combined with an astonishing musical talent soon enabled him to play the few songs that he knew. Tiring of these, he next tried making up tunes of his own, one of which he played for his friend, saying, "Maybe one day I'll be good enough to accompany you, Max."

"You haven't got it in you to be a musician," came the chilling reply. "Take my word for it, I can tell."

George Gershwin knew better. All his life, in fact, he was sure of himself musically, so much so that at times he laid himself open to the charge of being immodest. Yet history shows that musical giants such as Gershwin *are* confident. They feel the great talent that is within them. And without this feeling how would they have the power to push forward their music, demanding that it be heard, insisting to people, "Listen. Just listen. This is good. I know it's good. Only *listen!*"?

For more than two years George's musical life went on unknown to his family—not that it would have made much difference to them one way or the other. Mr. Gershwin, a mild-mannered, humorous man, was busy trying to provide for his family, which he did in a fairly successful, if restless, manner. He was forever buying and selling businesses: for a restaurant he would swap a stationery store; the restaurant, in turn, was traded for a bakery, the bakery for a rooming house, the rooming house for a Turkish bath. The only bother to the rest of the family was that Mr. Gershwin liked to live near his various businesses, so they were endlessly moving. In later years Ira remembered that they lived in twenty-eight apartments between 1900 and 1917.

One of the reasons that most of easygoing Mr. Gershwin's enterprises succeeded was that Mrs. Gershwin kept a sharp eye on the finances. She was as ambitious as he was casual. Beautiful and purposeful, she wanted her children to get ahead in the world, and it worried her that while Ira, the eldest, did well enough at school and loved reading George's marks were always poor and he seemed to care nothing about getting an education. It's possible that had she known about George's secret musical life she would have been suspicious that it kept him from doing his homework. But she didn't know, and in 1910, by accident, she gave George's musical education a tremendous boost for the most unmusical of reasons.

In that year, Mrs. Gershwin learned that her sister had purchased that symbol of prestige—a piano. Proud Mrs. Gershwin wasn't going to be outdone. The year 1910 had been a good one for her husband, and there was enough money to purchase a secondhand upright so that Ira, so said Mrs. Gershwin, might have some proper musical training. Imagine her astonishment when, as George Gershwin told the story later, "No sooner had it come through the window and been backed up against the wall, than I was at the keys." Where had George, the son who got bad marks in school and never concentrated on anything, learned music? Indeed, the whole family was impressed and Ira noted in particular how skillfully George used his left hand.

But obstacles still remained in the way of the musical training George now so badly wanted. Ira was the oldest and Ira had once been given a few sketchy piano lessons by his aunt. Therefore, reasoned Mrs. Gershwin, Ira would be the musician of the family. He was taken from the nickel novels that he loved to read and made to practice under the supervision of his aunt. With painful slowness he reached page 32 of a book of exercises while George stood by enviously. By this time Ira's aunt-teacher had decided that it was her fault that her nephew was making such poor progress and suggested hiring a professional teacher. Ira announced firmly that he refused to take piano lessons from a professional and banged down the cover of the piano. As he rose from the piano stool, his brother grabbed it—a place that George Gershwin was to keep for the rest of his life. A few days later, Miss Green, the teacher, came to give George his first lesson at the standard rate of fifty cents an hour.

Now he was a Maggie too.

2 / I'm On My Way

Many people think of a genius as a person with some kind of extraordinary creative ability. Frequently they forget that no genius ever left his mark on the world without having an equally extraordinary ability to persevere. Creative talent, alone, is not enough. It must be backed up by persistence, as Ralph Waldo Emerson well knew when he defined genius as "the infinite capacity for taking pains."

Today the world recognizes that George Gershwin was a musical genius. He might never have gained that recognition if, at the age of twelve, he had not pushed and struggled to gain knowledge of the language of music, in the face of a difficult and unusual handicap. Most of the world's great composers had some kind of musical background. Mozart and Beethoven, for instance, were taught music by their fathers. Other composers had parents who either played instruments or simply loved music enough to want to expose their children to it.

Not so George Gershwin. Though it was obvious how much music excited and fascinated the boy, no one in the Gershwin family paid any attention: not friendly, wisecracking Mr. Gershwin; not lively Mrs. Gershwin, who was already dreaming of a career as a bookkeeper for her boy George; not quiet, older brother Ira, deeply immersed in writing, editing and even printing by hand his own high-school newspaper, which he called *The Leaf*. The Gershwin family went as far as to think it a good thing for a tough boy like George, with his poor marks at school and his street fighting and even occasional petty stealing, to like anything as improving as playing the piano. They very willingly provided fifty cents a week for Miss Green to come and drill George in Beyer's book of musical exercises. But that was all.

For George it was simply not enough. In the vaudeville theaters and music halls, when the entertainers sang songs like "A Bicycle Built for Two" or "Put Your Arms Around Me," he wanted to know how such tunes were put together—perhaps, even, how he could write a song like that himself. And the new hit, "Alexander's Ragtime Band," that everyone was so crazy about, how had the composer, Irving Berlin, written down its jerky ragtime rhythms? And what about a great big orchestra with all the instruments playing different parts? He didn't even know the *names* of half of the instruments, let alone how anyone wrote for them. None of these things was he learning from Miss Green, nor from the new musical exercises which she mechanically assigned him each week.

So Gershwin rebelled. He demanded a new teacher. Miss Green was no good, he told his family. A new teacher was found, also at fifty cents an hour, a female teacher of exactly the same kind as Miss Green. Soon Gershwin let out another howl. Whereupon a third teacher was turned up, also a female, also charging fifty cents per hour.

George decided to take matters into his own hands. In the neighborhood there was a dramatic-looking Hungarian with long moustaches named Mr. Goldfarb. Mr. Goldfarb's manner of playing the piano was as theatrical as his appearance, and he looked so impressive as he rocked back and forth on the piano stool rolling his eyes and sighing during the tender parts of the melody that he could command $1.50 an hour for a lesson. For that amount of money, George decided, Mr. Goldfarb must be the finest teacher in the world, and he arranged to study with him. Pretty soon, George too was rocking back and forth on the piano stool and rolling *his* eyes and paying no more attention to the note values or rhythms of the music than his teacher did.

Fortunately, Gershwin's natural musical talent saved him. At the end of six months' study with Mr. Goldfarb he could play a long, quite difficult transcription of the *William Tell* Overture (and practically act out the story of the opera at the same time). But he instinctively knew that his teacher's approach to music was crude and vulgar.

About this time Gershwin made a new friend, Jack Miller, who was a pianist with an amateur symphony orchestra. To Miller, George poured out his troubles and his aspirations: if only he could find a really good teacher, one who not only taught the piano well, but who would explain to him about the different musical forms and the various instruments and advise him what concerts to go to and what musical artists to hear and——

Throughout his life, whenever Gershwin was talking about music, particularly himself in relation to music, he would get so excited and carried away that he could scarcely listen to what anyone else was saying. Now, through the flood of his own words, it came to him dimly that Jack Miller was also speaking—saying something about trying his teacher. "*Your* teacher?" George asked. Miller nodded.

His teacher was named Charles Hambitzer, Miller explained enthusiastically, and he was a professional musician who knew so much about music that he was able to teach piano, violin and cello. Hambitzer played regularly in the Waldorf-Astoria Orchestra and he was also a composer. Some of his compositions had actually been played in that most exalted of all auditoriums, Carnegie Hall on 57th Street! Hambitzer was a truly wonderful teacher, Miller said, and the next time he went for a lesson he would bring George along to meet the great man.

"But would he take anyone as raw as me?" asked George, a mixture of hope and fear showing in his dark eyes.

"He'll ask to hear you play and that will decide him."

"And don't his lessons cost a lot?" George went on, and with a sinking heart learned that Hambitzer charged, naturally, what a teacher of his worth was entitled to receive. "My family would never pay *that* much."

The next time Miller had a lesson with Charles Hambitzer he kept his word and took his thirteen-year-old friend, trembling with excitement and apprehension, to the studio. As expected, the teacher, a kindly, curly haired man, not at all frightening, waved Gershwin to the piano and told him to play something. Rubbing his hands together the boy dived into the overture to *William Tell,* complete with all the gestures and facial expressions and distorted playing that he had learned from Mr. Goldfarb. Hambitzer listened, worryingly silent throughout the performance, and only when the last violently struck note had died away did he get up from his chair and say, referring to Mr. Goldfarb, "Listen, let's hunt out that guy and shoot him—and not with an apple on his head either."

Despite the crudeness and exaggeration of Gershwin's playing Hambitzer had recognized the boy's talent and extreme seriousness. He would be glad to take George as a pupil, he announced. But the lessons were so expensive!

cried George, almost dismayed at being accepted—and his family didn't approve of his being a musician. They wanted him to become a bookkeeper. In that case, Hambitzer said with a smile, if George couldn't pay for the lessons he wouldn't charge him for them.

"I was just crazy about that man," Gershwin said of his new teacher later, and in gratitude he rounded up ten other pupils for him.

The lessons began and Hambitzer became more and more excited about the intense, musically ignorant boy with his tough, shy manner. "I have a new pupil who will make his mark in music if anybody will," he predicted a few weeks later in a letter to his sister. "The boy is a genius without a doubt; he's just crazy about music and can't wait until it's time to take his lesson. No watching the clock for this boy."

Now began a thrilling period as Hambitzer began to unlock door after door in the treasure-house of music, letting its riches spill forth. Discovery is thrilling for anyone who responds to music. Imagine what it was like for a genius like George Gershwin. Until his lessons with Hambitzer, harmony had been to him "a sort of instinctive feeling for tone combinations." Now, for the first time, he learned *why* some of the ways he had tried to use chords had been right or wrong and how to make them work most interestingly and effectively. Advised by Hambitzer, he began to attend concerts of the New York Philharmonic Society, the New York Symphony Society and by great pianists and violinists. For the first time he heard the winding, elaborately embroidered melodies of Chopin, the pounding folk rhythms of Liszt, the dreamy, murmurous harmonies of Debussy. He absorbed completely each new musical experience and stored it up like nourishment, as a young, wonderfully well-growing plant might in order one day to bear magnificent fruit.

In later years, when George Gershwin was asked how he had become such a marvelous pianist with so little piano instruction (four years, in all), he attributed it to his "habit of intensive listening. I had gone to concerts and listened not only with my ears, but with my nerves, my mind, my heart. I had listened so earnestly that I became saturated with the music . . . Then I went home and listened in memory."

As many youthful enthusiasts do, he began to keep a scrapbook. Into it went pictures of the great composers and of musicians that he admired, such as Josef Hofmann, Harold Bauer, and Josef Lhévinne (all, by no coincidence whatsoever, great pianists of the day), as well as his concert programs. Two in particular were given special places of honor: one was of a concert played by the Waldorf-Astoria Orchestra on Sunday, April 13, 1913, which included the first movement of the Rubinstein Piano Concerto in D Minor—"Soloist: Charles Hambitzer"; the other was of a violin recital five nights later at Cooper Union by "Master Max Rosenzweig." For the latter he even managed to get his whole family to turn out, including older brother Ira, now very grown up as an undergraduate at New York City College and a member of an august literary club.

Only on one point did Hambitzer and his young pupil disagree. As the teacher wrote to his sister, "He wants to go in for this modern stuff, jazz and what not. But I'm not going to let him for a while. I'll see that he gets a firm foundation in the standard music first."

The truth was that Hambitzer could not stop the boy from going in "for this modern stuff." It was too much around him. Despite the fact that radios did not exist and phonographs were primitive and expensive, all America was as enthusiastic about popular music as the country is today. Many families had an upright piano in the parlor, or if that was too expensive someone would at least learn to play the ukelele or the harmonica. New songs were published by the thousands every year and the sheet music of hits like "Let Me Call You Sweetheart" sold as many as eight million copies.

Popular music was a part of everyone's life. People would leave Broadway theaters humming and whistling the charming melodies from Victor Herbert's operettas or gather around the piano player in a saloon to roar out songs like "When You Wore a Tulip" and "My Gal Sal." Gershwin was four or five years old when ragtime became the rage in America. Its jerky, syncopated rhythms created a whole new style of piano playing and set couples to doing "daring" dances such as the one-step and the fox trot. In the same year that George was pasting up his scrapbook with concert programs and pictures of the great composers, a new kind of song called the blues swept the country. Its strange, sad mood seemed to be built out of a different kind of scale consisting of flatted "blue" sounding notes. About this time, too, word had begun to reach New York of a new kind of music that they were playing in New Orleans and Chicago: the men in the band didn't play a tune "straight" but put it through all kinds of rhythmic and melodic variations—sometimes all of them doing something different at the same time. They called this music jazz.

No one as responsive to music as young Gershwin could help feeling excited about what was going on in the world of popular music. To him it was America's music, more real than

Harold Bauer

Josef Hofmann

Two of the giant pianists whose pictures were included in George Gershwin's scrapbook. CULVER PICTURES, INC.

the formal symphonies and concertos and rhapsodies to which Hambitzer had introduced him. Not that he didn't think those works beautiful. It was only that they seemed more remote, more foreign, whereas the songs that he heard in the vaudeville theaters or pounded out by the hard-working song pluggers in department stores seemed to belong much more to his life. "In My Merry Oldsmobile," "For Me and My Gal" and "The Band Played On"—these were songs that expressed the situations and feelings of the world that he lived in. And the quick, nervous rhythms of ragtime and the new jazz expressed perfectly the hectic tempo of George's own home town, New York City.

To Gershwin, America's popular music was *his* music and, despite what Hambitzer and other musicians might think, was as important to him as the beautiful but impersonal compositions that he heard in the concert halls. And anyway, why should he have to choose between the two? He liked them both and if one day he became a composer, as he had begun to dream of doing, he saw no reason why he couldn't cross the style and rhythms of popular music with the forms of classical music. It was as simple as that.

Meanwhile, eager and ambitious to make use of his newly acquired knowledge of harmony, he set out to write a quartet. He got as far as the first movement, then, overcome with shyness at such daring, put it away and never showed it to his revered teacher. But music of a lighter kind, rags and one-steps and tangos, came quickly to his fingers and now, for the first time, he was able to write down what he had made up.

One day late in the winter of 1914 Ira Gershwin came home and announced that he had been put in charge of organizing an evening of entertainment for his college literary club. His first thought, naturally, had been of brother George, who could act as accompanist for the program. And perhaps George would like to play a solo of his own too. Gershwin was delighted at the idea. There was to be a printed program, Ira continued, and he would have to know what George was going to perform. Just put down "Piano Solo," was the reply.

The night of the entertainment arrived and George's solo turned out to be a lively and catchy tango which oddly enough no one seemed to have heard before. Had it just been published? he was asked later. Who was the composer? No, the tango had never been published, George replied and confessed that he was the composer. That night, for the first time in public, George Gershwin had played George Gershwin.

While Gershwin the musician made great strides forward, Gershwin the scholar waned. By the age of fourteen he had managed—but only just—to get a grammar-school certificate. In Mrs. Gershwin's opinion playing the piano and being interested in music was a very nice sideline, but it wasn't a way to make a living. George hadn't done too badly in mathematics. George would go to the High School of Commerce and study double-entry bookkeeping. When he graduated from high school he then would be able to get a job that paid maybe as much as fifteen dollars a week.

All through the winter of 1914 George toiled away at the dreary business of learning bookkeeping. At the same time, the lessons with Hambitzer, the concerts that he heard, his growing skill as a pianist were all combining to make the lure of music more and more irresistible. Music was his life. From the moment that he had stood transfixed outside the school window and heard Max Rosenzweig play the Dvořák

Humoresque he had known it. Music was like the air he breathed: he must take it in and give it out. Of this he was now certain.

With self-confidence that was typical of George Gershwin, the fifteen-year-old boy decided to take a bold step. Two months after his successful appearance at Ira's literary club, he came home one day and, taking a deep breath, announced that he had quit school for good. He was going into the music business. Then he dropped his head and waited for the storm to break.

Break it did. He couldn't quit school, raged Mrs. Gershwin. He must get himself an education. No one got ahead in the world without an education. Everybody knew that. Even if he didn't become a bookkeeper at least he could teach. He could always get a nice respectable job at a beginner's salary of perhaps eleven dollars a week.

A vagabond, Mr. Gershwin said mournfully. He'd always been afraid that was how George would turn out.

Besides, how could he earn money in the music business? Mrs. Gershwin went on. Everybody knew that musicians were always out of work and that composers starved. What kind of life was that?

George stood his ground and when the storm had somewhat abated announced quietly that not only was he going into the music business but that he had found a job. He was going to be a piano pounder for Remick's, the music publishers, at a salary of——

A piano pounder? shrieked Mrs. Gershwin. A piano pounder was no better than a bum, playing in low dives and off of trucks in the streets. Her George, a piano pounder?

——at a salary of *fifteen* dollars a week, George continued patiently, as much as a high-school graduate got on his first job. Mr. and Mrs. Gershwin stared in amazement at their son and were silent.

Robert Payne, one of Gershwin's biographers, has described him as he looked them: "A tall, well-built boy with brown eyes and hair brushed straight back from the forehead, deceptively mild until he sat down at the piano and then he played like an abandoned demon."

He was fifteen years old and he was on his way—the youngest song plugger in a very tough business.

3 / Slap That Bass

SPRING CAME ON in the year 1914 and the windows were left open in the brownstone houses that lined 28th Street off Fifth Avenue. Anyone who turned into the street expecting relief from the noise made by the primitive cars and trucks plying New York City's busiest thoroughfare found himself in the midst of an even worse racket. From the windows of almost every house poured a din of scrambled musical sounds —nasal-toned tenors and flutey sopranos, piping children and bellowing "old-time" singers, sentimental violins and brash accordions, banjos, trumpets, saxophones, harmonicas and, through it all, the relentless noise of perhaps thirty or forty pianos beating out one-steps and waltzes and fox trots and tangos from eight to ten hours a day. This was Tin Pan Alley, street of the music publishers and place of George Gershwin's first job.

No one knows who named Tin Pan Alley. It was not always on 28th Street but landed there after several moves as New York City spread uptown. The name, anyway, meant more than just a place. By 1914, when Gershwin, eager and confident for all his fifteen years, sat down before an upright piano in Remick's on 28th Street, Tin Pan Alley stood for a big, commercial musical operation in which the competition was stiff, the artistic standards nil and the profits (sometimes) enormous.

Today a singer (known or unknown) records a new song, then perhaps makes an appearance singing it on a television variety show. The disc jockeys move in and begin to plug the record, and with that curious element of luck which makes one song catch on with the public and another fail, the record may become a hit.

In 1914 Tin Pan Alley had more of a problem boosting a song into a hit. There was no radio or television—only vaudeville. Recording techniques were crude, and profits for publishers came not from record but sheet music sales. Yet how was the public to buy a song unless it had a chance to hear it?

This was where song plugging came in. Just as popular recording artists can often make a song a hit today, so could the vaudeville entertainers in 1914. And then, just as now, it worked both ways: a song sometimes made a star, and a star, a song. Each very much needed the other.

As a result, the entertainment world came crowding into Tin Pan Alley looking for new material from the music publishers, who, naturally, welcomed eagerly an Irish tenor wanting a new sentimental ballad for his Boston engagement, a pair of singing tap dancers in search of a "novelty" number to add to their act, a once-famous musical-comedy soprano out to find a song suitable for a comeback in vaudeville. And behind the rows of brownstone façades along 28th street, piano-pounding song pluggers like young George Gershwin were waiting for them.

They worked in cubicles made up of cardboardlike partitions. Gershwin's was the size of a not-very-large self-service elevator, with enough room for an upright piano, a stool, himself and one or two other people to whom he was out to sell the latest Remick's songs. This was his job—trying to

George Gershwin's first job was plugging songs for Remick's in Tin Pan Alley. CULVER PICTURES, INC.

convince each entertainer who came in, by a mixture of fast talking and good piano playing, that Remick's had the very number he was looking for.

The Irish tenor wants a new ballad? He has the very thing, says George, and begins to play a commonplace tune very cleverly, slipping a few references to old Irish folk songs into the bass. Of course, George continues, at the moment the words are about romantic Paris in the springtime, but there's no reason why they can't be changed to romantic Dublin in the springtime. And the song has a very Irish feeling to it, now doesn't it? That it has, agrees the tenor, and decides to take it. . . .

For the tap dancers' novelty number, Gershwin selects a fast-moving rag, which he pounds out with his strong arms in an irresistible beat that sets their feet moving automatically. It's fine for the dance part of their act, they tell him, but they need to be able to sing it, too, and it's too fast for that. Gershwin's hands slip back to the piano keys and he begins to hum a smooth little tune that seems vaguely familiar. What he has done is to halve the time of the rag and take out its syncopations. Now the tap dancers have exactly what they want. . . .

New problems arise with the once-famous musical-comedy soprano. He has exactly the thing for her, he says, a charming waltz with a lovely refrain all about "hollyhocks in a cottage garden." The soprano doesn't read music very well, but George manages to get her on the starting pitch and guide her through the melody. The "hollyhocks in a cottage garden" refrain soars to a high note but the once-famous soprano does not gain the necessary altitude. She is embarrassed and therefore annoyed. He must have started the song in too high a key, George says hastily, and transposes it half a tone down.

(He dares not put it lower; there is no bottom range left to her voice either.) This time all goes smoothly. The soprano, pleased with her accomplishment, decides the song is just what she is looking for and includes it in her act. . . .

Soon all three songs are being performed before the public and Remick's is selling hundreds of copies of each—thanks to Gershwin's skillful piano pounding.

Working as a song plugger was naturally invaluable to Gershwin's career. Being paid to play the piano all day was helpful enough; learning how songs were put together, how tempos and key changes could alter the effect of a tune, even more so. In addition, most of Tin Pan Alley's compositions were so utterly trite and mechanical that his musical imagination was challenged and he continually tried to play them with inventive and original touches.

Besides selling songs to professional entertainers, the song plugger had another side to his job: reaching the public directly. Pluggers were sent to local music shops and department stores to pound out the new tunes. They and their pianos were loaded on trucks and dispatched to various parts of the cities to peddle their wares to the crowds that gathered. In the evening, pluggers went into bars and cafés where the managers allowed them to sing and play to the patrons. Songs were plugged between events in sports arenas and in silent-movie theaters, where the words were flashed on the screen and everybody in the audience sang along. Another popular method of song boosting was to station a plugger in the balcony of a vaudeville theater. When the performer on stage had sung his number through, the plugger would rise to his feet, and, as if carried away by the impact of it, roar out the refrain, carrying the audience along with him. One who got his start doing this kind of song plugging was Irving Berlin, who by the time Gershwin was assigned his cubicle at Remick's on 28th Street had become a well-established composer and an idol of the fifteen-year-old youth.

Though he was young, the power and originality of Gershwin's playing soon began to be noticed. A young lyricist named Irving Caesar, who came to Remick's hoping to market some of his verses, stayed just to sit in Gershwin's cubicle and hear him play. "His rhythms had the impact of a sledge hammer. His harmonies were years ahead of the time. I had never before heard such playing of popular music."

Occasionally Gershwin would be sent down to work in Atlantic City, the popular seaside resort on the coast of New Jersey. It was a good place for song plugging. People came there for pleasure, to ride along the famous boardwalk in rolling wicker chairs and to enjoy the warm sea breeze blowing in off the Gulf Stream. They had the leisure to listen to a new song. Gershwin and his fellow song pluggers made their usual rounds—the music stores by day and the smaller restaurants and bars in the evening.

Afterward, a number of them would gather late at night in a restaurant on the boardwalk. With the salty night wind coming from the black Atlantic and the waves swishing beneath the pilings, they would talk on and on—the way people always do who are in the same line of work—about song plugging and the world of Tin Pan Alley. "I can still recall George's eagerness, his enthusiasm for his work, his passionate interest in every phase of the popular-music business," Harry Ruby, a song plugger from those Atlantic City days, remembered about Gershwin in later years. Ruby, who became a well-known composer of popular songs, as well as one of Gershwin's best friends, also quickly recognized the superiority of his piano playing. "As I look back upon it I can say it was a completely different world from ours, and we did not completely understand it at the time, though we all reacted to it instinctively."

In what way his musical world differed from that of the other song pluggers was probably not very clear then even to Gershwin. It seemed to center around the fact that most of them regarded popular music as a business, as a means of making a living—and sometimes a very good one at that. But to Gershwin popular music, while also important to his making a living, was something he believed in passionately. To him it was the people's music, the folk music of America.

By the time Gershwin first got his job as a song plugger, America was a firmly united nation, criss-crossed by railroads and telephones and generously dotted with large cities in all sections of the land. Yet in some ways it was still a young nation, rather like a hulking young man from the country, just come of age, who is eager to deepen and mature, but is still slightly self-conscious and unsure of himself in the matter of such refinements as the arts. True, by 1914 America could point with great pride to her writers and poets: Hawthorne, Poe, Emerson, Whitman, Melville, Mark Twain, Henry James —the list was brilliant and varied. She had given birth to two remarkable painters: Whistler, whom she had lost to Europe, and Eakins, who had stayed behind. But when it came to music, America had not produced one composer of comparable rank—not so much as a single great piece of music.

Why this mysterious failure?

In some extraordinary way, the fifteen-year-old Gershwin understood the reason. By now he knew some of the world's great music—Beethoven's Third Symphony, for example, the "Eroica." And what was the lilting melody of the last movement which Beethoven put through so many fascinating variations? Nothing but a dance tune, a *contredanse,* which Beethoven in the popular dance style of the time had written a few years before, but which sounded perfectly appropriate in a symphony. Gershwin had also heard the mazurkas and polonaises of Chopin, complex piano pieces full of astonishing elaborations and subtle contrasts. Yet what were they but works built entirely on popular dance rhythms of Chopin's native Poland? He had heard themes of Tchaikovsky which recalled the melancholy folk songs of Russia and the rhapsodies of Liszt which were based on the now-somber, then-fiery rhythms of Hungarian folk music.

Folk music! This was the answer, Gershwin had realized. All the great European composers had derived inspiration—sometimes actual themes—from the folk music of their native countries. But the few American composers whose works had been performed up to that time thought of symphonies and concertos and operas as a slightly foreign kind of music just the way Gershwin did. As a result, Americans who wanted to become serious composers always believed that they must study in Europe, and they ended up writing compositions that were pale imitations of European works. They had turned their backs on what should have been their basic source of inspiration—their own native American music.

And what an extraordinary source it is! No other country possesses anything like it. Historians have pointed out that since the world began never has there been such a mass migration as the settling of America. Equally, never was there such a migration and merging of different kinds of folk music as was poured into the famous American melting pot.

Into it went English ballads and sentimental airs from Scotland, Irish reels and Central European polkas, mournful

Slavic melodies and chattering Spanish dances, France, Italy, Poland, the Scandinavian countries all contributed their special songs and dances. To this varied brew was added the most unique and piquant flavor of all, African music contributed by the Negro when he was brought to American shores in chains.

In the misery of the Negro's state, music was his one consolation. Of the God he had been taught to worship he sang spirituals, his own versions of the hymns that the Pilgrims had originally brought to America. Of his personal troubles he sang sad songs using a limited flatted scale which came to be called blues. To lighten his load and shorten the day he sang work songs. And on those occasions when he was briefly released from sorrow, his happiness took flight in wild songs and "shouts" and dances based on complex rhythmic variations that were a part of his African heritage. These irregular, syncopated rhythms, this free, endlessly varied way of performing music combined with all the other ingredients in the pot, and the result was a folk music of enormous range and richness, with a special flavor that can only be called American.

"It is not always recognized that America has folk music," George Gershwin wrote in an interview a number of years later, "yet it really has not only one but many different folk musics . . . all having validity and being a possible foundation for development into art-music." Probably he didn't use quite such long words to express his ideas on the importance of America's popular music when he talked about them late at night in the restaurant on the boardwalk. Even so, his ideas worried his friends slightly. "When he spoke of the artistic mission of popular music," Harry Ruby remembered later, "we thought he was going high falutin'. The height of artistic achievement to us was a pop song that sold lots of copies and we just didn't understand what he was talking about."

That cynicism of Tin Pan Alley never rubbed off onto George Gershwin. All his life he was to make money out of music, but never by putting anything over on the public that was mechanical or second rate. He had a kind of musical perfectionism which even the critics who called him "commercial," could not gainsay. It was this perfectionism that Gershwin's teacher, Charles Hambitzer had recognized the day the boy walked into his studio.

Despite his grueling schedule as a piano pounder, Gershwin managed to continue studying with his kindly, curly-haired teacher, and the following year Hambitzer recommended that he also take lessons in theory and advanced harmony from a colleague in the Waldorf-Astoria Orchestra named Edward Kilenyi. Soon Gershwin was leading a very strange musical existence indeed: one moment knocking out cheap Tin Pan Alley ditties, the next, analyzing how the four voices moved in a Bach chorale; sometimes playing for the most musically ignorant show people, other times working with superbly trained musicians who had the highest reverence for musical art.

Gershwin's studies with Kilenyi were extremely important to his career. For the first time, he learned about the instruments of the orchestra, how to write for them and how to combine them in various ways to achieve a wide range of musical color. Gershwin's exercise books from his studies with Kilenyi still exist. David Ewen, another of Gershwin's biographers, writes in his *Journey to Greatness* that "they reveal how meticulous he was in being accurate and correct, how fastidious he was about neatness. They also betray the fact that once he learned the basic rules Gershwin often tried to work out his personal ideas in direct opposition to established practice. In this he was encouraged by his teacher."

Kilenyi also encouraged Gershwin to write popular music. Aware that most American composers had great difficulty in getting their works performed, he thought that if Gershwin made a great popular success, conductors would be more interested in programming serious compositions that he might write.

Backed by this notion and situated as he was in the heart of Tin Pan Alley, what was more natural for Gershwin than to begin to write songs of his own? And what more natural than to play them to his boss, Mose Gumble, the president of Remick's? Gumble's reaction was crushing. Gershwin was a piano pounder, he said, and when he wanted new songs he had a whole list of composers on his payroll to get them from. And these were too sentimental anyway.

Undaunted, Gershwin decided to try another publisher. Irving Berlin was a composer he particularly admired (later he would refer to him as "America's Franz Schubert"), and Irving Berlin had recently started his own music-publishing business. Boldly Gershwin stormed the new offices and played his songs for the famous composer. Then, tense with hope and excitement, he waited for the verdict. Very good, full of talent, said Berlin. Gershwin held his breath. Were they going to be accepted? Yes, Berlin continued, he was certain that young Gershwin had the makings of a fine career ahead of him. What he needed to do was to keep working. . . . Write more songs, lots more. . . . Listen to the songs of other composers. . . .

Sadly, Gershwin gathered up his manuscripts and with a word of thanks left the office.

He hardly needed to be told to listen to other composers' songs, hearing them as he did with the same concentration that he gave to music of the great composers. About this time Gershwin's Aunt Kate was married, and at the wedding reception the band played a tune which sent him dashing across the room to find out its name and composer. The song, he learned, was called "You're Here and I'm Here" and it was by a man named Jerome Kern. Another song by the same composer followed, smooth, inventive, with a chorus that was suddenly and unconventionally lengthened in its last repetition. When he compared these two songs with the average Remick product, Gershwin began to realize how hackneyed and mechanical Tin Pan Alley's music really was. What could you expect of song writers so musically ignorant that they picked out their tunes with one finger on the piano? But Jerome Kern, Gershwin instantly realized, was a real musician. Kern became Gershwin's second idol, joining Irving Berlin, and remained so for all his life.

Write more songs, Irving Berlin had advised him. It seemed like wise counsel. Gershwin had met a young lyricist named Murray Roth and the two decided to collaborate. Gershwin knocked out a jaunty rag made up of quick, short phrases and Roth thought up some lines to fit them.

When you want 'em
You can't get 'em,
When you've got 'em
You don't want 'em . . .[1]

"'Em," naturally, referred to the female sex, which had been mentioned in the verse.

One of the up-and-coming entertainers who often came to

[1] Used by permission of Harry Von Tilzer Music Publishing Company.

Remick's was the now-famous "Red Hot Mama" singer, Sophie Tucker. Hoping that his boss wouldn't catch him plugging a non-Remick product, Gershwin played and sang his new song to her. Good enough to publish, was her prompt verdict, and she would recommend it. Not to Remick's, Gershwin said hastily, not to his boss, Mose Gumble, who thought of him as only a piano pounder. No, not Remick's, said Sophie Tucker, but to another firm headed by her good friend Harry Von Tilzer.

Sophie Tucker's recommendation to Von Tilzer was enough, and at the age of eighteen Gershwin became a published composer. Holding a copy of his song just off the press, he felt that at last he was on his way to fame—and to riches. (Money, Gershwin always realized from a childhood of doing without, was an extremely useful thing to have around.) Hence his scorn of the arrangement that Murray Roth, the lyricist, had made with Von Tilzer to sell out his interest in the song for an advance of fifteen dollars. To Gershwin, ever confident of his own music, this was plain foolishness. He refused to sell out his interest and waited instead for the royalties from it to pile up. Finally, after sufficient time had passed, Gershwin went around to Von Tilzer's office to collect the large sum of money that he was sure must be waiting for him. The publisher put a single bill into Gershwin's outstretched hand. It was a five-dollar bill—all that the composer ever earned for his first published song.

Still, if one song had been good enough to print, surely he could write another. Again with Murray Roth, he turned out a little number in two-four time which the famous Sigmund Romberg, composer of operettas, accepted for a Broadway show of which he was musical director. A Gershwin song on

Sophie Tucker, an up-and-coming young singer in 1915, was responsible for George Gershwin's first song being published.

CULVER PICTURES, INC.

Broadway! That seemed like real progress. More and more George felt attracted to Broadway anyway.

The fact was that he had begun to tire of song plugging and what he called the "popular song racket." Whatever novelty there had been in it for him had long since worn off. All that remained was the offensively common tunes and stale harmonies which he had been pounding out for over two years. Suddenly he realized that he could stand them no more. With no idea of what his next step might be, he walked into the boss's office—and quit.

"Where are you going? What are you going to do?" asked Gumble, who had, after all, given George his first chance.

"I don't know," replied the young composer. "Something is taking me away."

What that "something" was he himself didn't quite know. Part of it was the hope of getting nearer to Broadway, with its more original and creative songs of the kind that Jerome Kern wrote. Another part was his still vague but perfectly real dream of one day writing serious compositions derived from America's popular music—an ambition that he could never realize if he stayed on in that mechanical music factory called Tin Pan Alley.

Walking out of Remick's onto 28th Street, George Gershwin rounded the corner and left Tin Pan Alley forever. His destination? He did not know. His future? Total uncertainty.

4 / I'll Build a Stairway to Paradise

A VAGABOND. THAT was what Mr. Gershwin had predicted his dark-haired, dark-eyed piano-playing son would become. Never did the prediction seem more ominously near the truth than in 1917 and 1918. At least for the past two years George had held a steady job. Even if it *was* in the music business it had brought in a regular fifteen dollars a week. Now he had thrown it away with some silly excuse about wanting to get closer to Broadway. Broadway was just another name for show business, and everyone knew what that meant—a knockabout, vagabond life, always on the road, living out of suitcases and off of chocolate bars or else cooking up terrible meals on burners that were smuggled into hotel rooms against the rules of the management. Vaudeville acts, whole shows even, were constantly closing up out of town, and crooked agents were forever running off with the week's admissions, leaving everyone stranded in the middle of nowhere without the price of a railroad ticket home.

It was all very worrying to Mr. and Mrs. Gershwin. And on top of that, their firstborn son, bespectacled, bookish Ira, who had showed some signs of becoming a well-educated citizen, maybe even a teacher, had just quit college after two years—just because he couldn't pass freshman mathematics. They didn't think it a bit funny, either, when he pointed out that obviously the only way he would ever get a diploma was to stay in college long enough to earn one by squatter's rights. Why couldn't the two boys stick with something and really work at it? There seemed to be a deep strain of restlessness in them both.

Within a month after leaving Remick's, George came home and triumphantly announced that he had found a new job, this time at a salary of twenty-five dollars a week. Say what his parents would about show business there was money in it, he pointed out proudly. His new job was at Fox's City Theater, right in the neighborhood. Maybe 14th Street wasn't Broadway, but it lay in that direction—and Fox's was well known for its good vaudeville shows, presented on a continuous basis afternoon and evening. Gershwin's job was to relieve the men in the orchestra during the supper show while they went out to eat. He was to be a kind of one-man band at the piano—his biggest opportunity!

Eager, but slightly nervous, George showed up at rehearsals the following Monday morning and sat in the orchestra pit throughout the afternoon, watching the acts and studying the accompaniments which he would soon have to play. No need for him to worry, he kept reminding himself, just as long as he had a good idea of the general routine of the show. With the music in front of him he was perfectly safe. He could read anything at sight, after all, and transpose into any key necessary.

The supper show came around. The men in the band laid down their instruments and George went to the piano to take over. For the first three or four acts all went well; one, which used some familiar Remick songs, was particularly successful because he could throw in some favorite embellishments from his days in the cubicle on 28th Street. Then a new act began, a typical vaudeville number, featuring a smiling leading lady, a smiling leading man, six smiling chorus girls—and a comedian whose face Gershwin was to remember with hatred and horror for the rest of his life. Reading from a battered, rather indistinct music manuscript George banged out the introduction to the chorus girls' opening song and very soon found that he was playing one tune and they were singing another. Anxiously he peered at the much penciled, confusingly marked score. Where *were* they? What cue had he missed? His face went hot. Fox's was in his neighborhood. Suppose there were friends in the audience—maybe even his skeptical parents? If only he hadn't gone around telling everyone about his big new job in show business.

Bravely George kept on, trying to improvise some kind of accompaniment to what the girls were singing. Suddenly, from across the footlights came the nasty voice of the comedian. Glaring and revealing as the beam of a searchlight, it was directed straight at George. "Hey—who told you you were a piano player? You ought to be banging a drum." The comedian gave a jeering laugh and the audience tittered. Completely unnerved, Gershwin dropped his hands from the piano. With the audience in on the joke, the comedian saw an opportunity to have some fun. Moving closer to the footlights he began to make merciless cracks about raw pianists who couldn't play the piano and vaudeville acts without music. The chorus girls giggled, the audience roared, while George, sensitive for all his musical self-confidence, sat helpless and humiliated.

Somehow, he managed to finish out the rest of the show. Then he fled. Nothing the manager could say—"Forget it," "It could happen to anyone"—would console him. His high-priced job in show business had lasted exactly one day.

Show business. The very expression became a nightmare to Mr. and Mrs. Gershwin. The next thing they knew Ira had gotten a job as cashier to, of all things, a traveling carnival show. Banging around the Midwest, he earned a living by totaling the take from people who paid to see the freaks, the "imported Oriental dancers," the tightrope walkers and the Wild West troupe featured in Colonel Lagg's Great Empire Show—"We do not tolerate immoral shows or gambling devices."

And just when Ira realized that this was no kind of life for him, George was off again, this time as accompanist to a vaudeville singer named Louise Dresser on the Keith circuit. True, the Keith circuit was the most famous in America and George claimed the job would give him experience in gauging audiences and all the other little tricks of showmanship, but as soon as the engagement was over, he'd be out of work again. Where was there any permanency for the two boys?

Back in New York, Ira continued his vagabond ways, wandering from job to job—darkroom assistant to a photographer, worker in the receiving department of a big store, reviewer of vaudeville shows for a small magazine—and, in his spare moments, turning out occasional sketches and some light verse. These he occasionally submitted to newspapers and magazines. His all-time return record was made during this period when he sent a poem to a paper at five o'clock in the evening and had it back with the rejection slip at seven forty-five the next morning.

While working as cashier at a Turkish bath in which his father had a part interest, however, Ira showed one of his sketches to a well-known dramatist who lived in one of the rooms above the bath. The dramatist thought it good enough to send to the magazine *Smart Set,* edited by two men famous in the literary world, H. L. Mencken and George Jean Nathan. They published it in the February, 1918, issue under the pseudonym Bruskin Gershwin. This was Ira's first published work:

THE SHRINE

Fascinated, he would stand before it, glorying. At such times, a sublime, shivery sensation . . . an incomprehensive wonder at the beauty of it all. Reverent before it, he felt invigorated with the spirit of eternal youth and happiness. Such soul-absorbing devotion to the embodiment of an ideal was unprecedented.

And one day it lay shattered in a thousand sharp, jagged fragments.

Panic-stricken, ashen-hued, he was scarcely able to mutter, "Gawd! Seven years' bad luck." [1]

It was a great honor, naturally, to be published by H. L. Mencken and George Jean Nathan though, financially, the rewards could not be described as enormous. For his sketch he received the sum of one dollar. Not long after, however, the humor magazine *Life* paid him twelve dollars for a verse. Writing verse, in fact, was something that had begun to interest Ira very much—verses for songs, that is—and in his quiet, apparently casual way he began turning out some practice lyrics, carefully keeping the secret from his family. George, after all, had invaded the songwriting field; Ira did not want it thought that he was copying his younger brother. And if his parents discovered that he had ambitions toward that most loathsome of enterprises—show business—he knew what their reaction would be.

Show business, however, had begun to do slightly better by George. The tour with Louise Dresser had provided val-

[1] Reprinted by permission of Mr. Ira Gershwin.

uable experience in performing before audiences, and he next landed a job as rehearsal pianist for a show called *Miss 1917*. Part of its score had been written by Jerome Kern, and Gershwin found himself working with his idol—and on Broadway at that.

In those days putting a Broadway musical together was a fairly routine business. The audience expected (and got) a star whose talents would be displayed to advantage, a love story of a not very believable kind, comedy with all the subtlety of a water-pistol fight—and the inevitable chorus line. Or sometimes Broadway put on musicals which were simply a series of numbers without a plot, suspiciously like vaudeville except that they were thought to be more sophisticated and were therefore called "revues." Nonetheless, Gershwin's new job gave him his first experience with what was to become his greatest love, the musical theater, and he made the most of the opportunity.

During breaks between rehearsing the chorus or working with the stars, George would sometimes play an impromptu piano recital for anyone who happened to be around. Then a hush would fall over the theater; the toughest, most knowing people in show business—from the company manager down to the last girl in the chorus line—came under the spell of his playing. At the piano the quiet, genial nineteen-year-old youth seemed to radiate a strange power. There was something almost supernatural about it.

Around this time three more of Gershwin's songs were published, one by his old firm, Remick's. It was gratifying to be acknowledged at last as a proper composer, not a piano pounder. It was also gratifying to know that his experience and reputation were growing simultaneously in the uneasy world of show business. Even so, his position could only be described as humble and uncertain in the extreme. He stood at the bottom of a long stairway with steps that were slippery and treacherously varied in height.

Then, from out of the blue, came an offer which seemed destined to change his life. Irving Berlin recently had been amazed by the way that Gershwin had been able to take down in writing one of Berlin's ragtime tunes and then play it back to him. Now the famous composer needed an arranger and musical secretary and offered Gershwin the job.

A chance to work with America's leading songwriter—and at an excellent salary! It seemed too good to be true. Then, to Gershwin's utter amazement, he heard Berlin say that he, personally, advised him *not* to take the job. Berlin might need Gershwin, but the question was did Gershwin need Berlin? "You're more than the skilled arranger that I'm looking for. You're a natural-born creator," said Berlin. "This sort of job would cramp you. You're meant for big things."

Coming from a composer whom Gershwin rated so highly, these were words to speed the beating of his heart. But to turn down the opportunity of working with Berlin, of meeting the "greats" in show business, of earning a steady, generous salary—how could he ever explain it to his family?

Of the many demands made on a creative genius, one of the most exacting is that in order to fulfill himself he must stand apart from others. He remains always a solitary figure, often a lonely one, who can, to be sure, take inspiration from other figures in his field, but never mold his own creative ideas to suit theirs. This has been true of all the great composers—Bach, Beethoven, Berlioz, Wagner, Stravinsky—and it is true of Gershwin. Young as he was, he realized the truth of Irving Berlin's words. He must go forward on his own, free of any other composer's dominating influence. Regretfully, he declined the offer.

As it turned out, integrity was its own reward. Soon after, he received a mysterious telephone call from Max Dreyfus, the important music publisher who had discovered Jerome Kern. Dreyfus explained that he had heard a lot about Gershwin from a friend, the company manager of *Miss 1917,* the show for which Gershwin had been rehearsal pianist. Would Gershwin call around at the office for a little talk?

The interview proved to be equally strange. Dreyfus had never even heard any of Gershwin's songs—nor did he ask him to play them now. He merely leaned back in his chair, his head cocked to one side, and sized up the youth as George talked excitedly about the music he hoped to write. Dreyfus was a gambler; he followed his intuitions. Sometimes they led him to failure; others, as when he had commissioned a little-known composer of piano pieces to write the music for an operetta called *The Firefly,* they brought him immense success. Gershwin's eagerness and intensity impressed him. "I feel you have some good stuff in you," he finally said to the young composer. "It'll come out. It may take months, it may take a year, it may take five years, but I'm convinced the stuff is there." Dreyfus paused dramatically. What could he be driving at? George wondered to himself. "I'll tell you what I'm willing to do; I'll gamble on you. I'll give you thirty-five dollars a week without any set duties. Just step in every morning and say hello. The rest will follow."

Patrons have often played an important part in the lives of composers. Haydn, Beethoven and Tchaikovsky all benefited from the generosity of wealthy people who admired their music sufficiently to help them to compose free of financial cares. Mozart's tragedy was that he never found such a benefactor. As a music publisher, Dreyfus, by subsidizing George Gershwin, hoped eventually to make money out of his songs. Nevertheless, the effect was the same. Now Gershwin could give his time to what he liked, could compose, play, study, develop musically without having to devote his energy to some unlikable job. He was secure. He would never have to worry again—except about how to become a better composer and musician.

As for clever Max Dreyfus, his hunch was eventually to bring him staggering profits.

A salaried composer of songs, George's most pressing need now was to find good lyricists. One obvious choice was Irving Caesar, who had admired his piano playing in the Remick days. Another, Gershwin found harder to get used to. Eighteen months and totally different temperaments separated him from his brother, Ira. Ira was so deliberate in everything he did, and so reticent—never pushing himself ahead the way dynamic, restless George did. Practically the last person George could have conceived of writing songs with was his own *brother*. Yet now he discovered that Ira had turned out some promising lyrics and planned to write more. It was impossible just to ignore the fact.

One of Ira's inspirations that caught George's fancy was a bouncy, irregular verse beginning, "The Great American Folk Song is a rag. . . ." "So," as Ira Gershwin reported to his diary of the time, "we sat down on (at, rather), the piano & Geo. started something. Something sounded good so we kept it. It was a strain for the 1st 2 lines. That in our possession we went along and Geo. developed the strain along legitimate or illegitimate (if you prefer) rag lines and with a little editing here & there the chorus, musical, stood forth in all its gory. [*sic*] But unhappily, the musical lines were of different lengths from the lyrics, so after having sweated & toiled & moiled over 20 or so different versions, it now devolves upon me to start an entirely new one keeping the 1st 2 lines as a memento of a tussle strenuous and an intimation of a struggle heroic to materialize." [2] It is a typical description of how the brothers Gershwin were to write many of their songs.

Thanks to Ira's patience a new version finally did materialize out "of a struggle heroic." Only now the beginning of the chorus went "The *real* American Folk Song is a rag." Soon afterward, a famous singing star of the day, Nora Bayes, became interested in using some other Gershwin songs for a new show, and when he played her this joint Gershwin effort she decided to use it too. Impressed by Gershwin's playing, she also hired him to accompany her.

The show, *Look Who's Here,* opened in Trenton, New Jersey, and Ira put on a mottled green tweed suit and a purple shirt and took the train down for the opening. Too shy to ask instructions, he got off at the wrong stop and only by dint of a wild trolley ride across the stretches of New Jersey managed to arrive for the first performance of the first all-Gershwin song. Not that the program said so. Modest Ira, afraid that he might appear to be cashing in on what he considered the glory of George's name, had taken a new pseudonym—Arthur Francis, derived from the first names of his younger brother and sister.

From Trenton *Look Who's Here* went to Pittsburgh, where it played to enthusiastic audiences. Among them was a music-struck youth who had bought a ticket to hear Nora Bayes but became fascinated instead by the playing of her accompanist. "I had never heard such brisk, unstudied, com-

[2] Reprinted by permission of Mr. Ira Gershwin.

pletely free and inventive playing, all within a consistent framework," he was to write of it later. This was the wise-cracking pianist Oscar Levant, who became one of Gershwin's closest friends as well as best interpreters.

An accompanist who steals attention from the star singer is comparable to a brightly burning fuse leading straight to a keg of gunpowder. Tension between the attractive but temperamental Miss Bayes and Gershwin began to mount. One day she asked him to change the ending of one of his songs. Gershwin refused. How dared he? she stormed. How dared a mere kid, a minor—not even twenty-one—refuse to do what she wanted, when great composers like Irving Berlin and Jerome Kern would always change their music to suit her? "I like this the way it is," Gershwin said calmly—and quit.

Show business. These were Gershwin's apprentice years. No one came to know it better than he did—the tensions, the egos, the backstage clashes, the crises, the sudden rocketlike rise of a new star, the poignant descent of an old one. Late in the fall of 1918, with America still rejoicing over the signing of the Armistice ending World War I, occurred one of George Gershwin's wildest adventures in show business.

It all began because Max Dreyfus was a gambler. Into his office had come an energetic, fast-talking young man named Perkins, who was putting together a revue built around "some songs and special effects" that he had brought from Paris. The famous comedian Joe Cook and his troupe had agreed to star in it, together with twenty-five colored musicians from the famous Chef Club, went on the young man, scarcely taking time to draw breath, and he'd lined up a nifty bunch of cuties for the chorus. If Dreyfus would put up enough money to open the show and find him a good composer to write five more songs for it, *Half Past Eight* (as he had named his gift to the entertainment world) would be the hit of the season. Dreyfus knew nothing of Perkins, but such enthusiasm was irresistible to him. Not only did he agree to put up the advance for the revue, but also to pay for the necessary orchestrations. As for a composer, Dreyfus knew the very man. His name was George Gershwin and he was eager to write for the theater . . .

Excitedly, George Gershwin wrote the necessary five songs and soon after, a tryout of *Half Past Eight* was planned in Syracuse, New York. Playbills went up around the city announcing the forthcoming show—the stars, the lovely chorus girls, the "additional songs by George Gershwin." A local organization bought out the house for the opening night. It looked as if Gershwin was about to hit the big time. There is a photograph of him taken at this time showing the proud, absurdly youthful musical-comedy composer, his face eager and sensitive above his stiff collar and natty chesterfield.

When Gershwin got to Syracuse, he discovered to his amazement that there wasn't any chorus line. He rushed to the producer and demanded an explanation. Budget problems—Perkins stammered nervously. He had been forced to economize. But what was a show without a chorus line? Gershwin protested. They *had* to have a chorus line for the finale—the customers would expect one. With youthful presence of mind he came up with an idea. How about dressing up the comedians in Joe Cook's troupe in floppy Chinese pajamas and giving them umbrellas to hold in front of their faces? They could do a couple of bends and kicks and twirl their pretty umbrellas, and when the curtain came down who in the audience would ever know the terrible truth?

George Gershwin at age twenty.

NEW YORK PUBLIC LIBRARY PICTURE COLLECTION, MUSIC DIVISION

Brilliant! Perkins agreed and dashed off to get the necessary costumes—and the umbrellas.

Despite its title, the curtain went up on *Half Past Eight* at quarter to nine. As a result of the producer's economical habits, the two halves of the show ran an inadequate forty-five minutes each and the numbers ranged from routine to depressing. Nor could George's five songs be described as memorable. By the time the finale was reached, the audience was thoroughly bored and disgruntled.

Then, in gaudy loose-fitting pajamas and clutching their furled umbrellas, on came the comedians, heads down, their backs to the audience. At a cue from the orchestra they were to open the umbrellas, conceal their faces and whirl around to the front. The cue sounded. The umbrellas flapped and the chorus of "lovelies" turned.

Alas! Perkins again had proved to be consistent in character. Since he had stinted on the chorus line, what reason was there to suppose he wouldn't economize on the umbrellas? Three of them failed to open and Perkins and his chorus of "lovelies" were seen for what they were. The curtain fell amid a storm of hisses and boos.

Not worth the tax on the tickets, was one critic's scathing opinion of *Half Past Eight* the next day. Nevertheless, it staggered on, but Perkins' saving ways had begun to worry certain members of the cast. Wasn't there a strong possibility that he might further economize, perhaps fail to pay their salaries at the end of the week? Just before the Wednesday matinee one of the acts refused to go on unless it was paid immediately. That was illegal, blustered Perkins. Salaries were to be paid at the end of the week as provided by contract. No money—no act, came the reply. Faced with the possibility of having to pay out money, the producer never wavered in his decision: no act.

Just at that moment Gershwin walked in. Depressed by the reception of this, his first show, he had not bothered to shave nor have his suit pressed. Perkins seized him. George must save the day and fill in for the deserting act. He must go out and play some of his hits while the scene was being changed for the next number. What hits? Gershwin asked himself gloomily. But if Perkins wanted him to fill in, he never minded playing for people. A few minutes later the handful of people in the theater were absolutely baffled to see a sloppy-looking youth come out of the wings, sit at the piano and bang out a medley of tunes that they had never heard before and then disappear.

It was perhaps the only time that George Gershwin ever played in public and received no applause.

Half Past Eight had opened on a Monday; it managed to last till Friday. Then, like an unwanted tramp, it was run out of town and never seen again. Gershwin had been promised fifteen hundred dollars for his five songs, but Perkins made one final economy move, and all the composer ever got was his train fare back to New York.

Show business. The people in it either learn to bounce back from failure or don't survive. In Syracuse George had struck a new, gloom-making low in his career. But several months later two of his latest songs were interpolated into a successful Broadway show and he signed a contract to write the entire score for a show of his own.

To be sure, the contract was with another unknown young producer named Alex Aarons and one would have expected

Gershwin to be wary of smooth-talking strangers who wanted to break into show business. Yet there was something about Aarons that inspired confidence, not only his formal-looking pince-nez and courteous manner which bespoke a different, more solid kind of person than usually turned up in that tinselly world, but also his impressive knowledge of music and sensitive response to it. His father was an amateur composer and wealthy businessman. Aarons had studied music and now wanted to devote the family fortune to producing better, more sophisticated Broadway musicals. Aarons' father had advised him to hire Victor Herbert to write the music for his first show, but Aarons, recognizing the subtle and original touches that had begun to appear in Gershwin's songs, had signed the completely unknown nineteen-year-old instead.

From the very beginning the musical communication between Aarons and Gershwin was most unusual. Ira Gershwin recalls in his witty and informative *Lyrics on Several Occasions* that "Alex was fond at the time of at least twenty of George's tunes which had not yet been written up lyrically, so he had no means of calling for any one of them by numeral or title. But he could request what he wanted to hear this way: Whisking his hand across George's shoulder he would say: 'Play me the one that goes like *that.*' Or: 'Play the tune that smells like an onion.' Or: '*You* know, the one that reminds me of the Staten Island ferry.' And so on. Though this mutual understanding didn't develop between them at their first meeting, it didn't take too long. I met Alex a few weeks after George did and in Alex's apartment heard five or six requests in this oblique manner." [3]

Aarons' show was called *La La Lucille,* and its first tryout town was Atlantic City. Gershwin found himself back in the

[3] Reprinted by permission of Mr. Ira Gershwin.

haunts of his song-plugging days, strolling on the boardwalk past the restaurant where he had once talked of his strange dream of writing serious American music. In the two years since he had been there last, much had changed. The day of the song plugger was beginning to darken. More and more, phonograph records were becoming the song pluggers of the time. As for Gershwin, he had become a Broadway composer and friend to the greats of the entertainment world like the famous lyricist B. G. DeSylva, who wrote the words for some of the songs in *La La Lucille,* and the famous singer Al Jolson, whom Gershwin met in Atlantic City during the tryout.

From Atlantic City the show went to Boston. "Vivacious . . . surprising of detail . . . harmoniously pleasing," wrote Brooks Atkinson, who was soon to become famous as drama critic of *The New York Times.* And when *La La Lucille* came to New York City late in the spring of 1919, the New York critics agreed with his verdict. No one thought it highly original or particularly sensational, but the show had charm and humor, they said, and this was enough for it to last for 104 performances through the heat of the summer and an actors' strike.

Show business. It is the most fickle and faithless of worlds. If a composer makes a moderate success, as Gershwin did with *La La Lucille,* he is called promising. If he comes up with a hit, his name is on everyone's lips as America's top composer. If his next show fails, he is dismissed as a washout. As Gershwin himself once said bitterly, "They forget everything you've done when you make one mistake." *La La Lucille* promised a future for Gershwin but did not assure it. That depended on what he did next.

The year 1919 brought with it a new trend in the entertainment world—the increasing popularity of the silent movies. Hollywood was booming as never before, and stars like Rudolph Valentino, Paula Negri and Douglas Fairbanks were rocketing to fame. The war was over and people were anxious to forget it, losing themselves amid the huge, exotic presences flashed before their eyes in the darkness of the movie theater.

As lush and immense as the images on the screen were some of the movie palaces built at this time. Along Broadway these theaters offered not only the latest Hollywood attraction but an elaborate stage show as well. When the sumptuous new Capitol Theater at Broadway and 51st Street opened its doors on October 24, 1919, the stage show included two of George Gershwin's latest songs. One in particular, the producer was sure, would be a hit; sixty chorus girls with light bulbs glowing on their shoes danced it on a darkened stage, singing,

> Swanee,
> How I love you, how I love you
> My dear old Swanee . . .

Outside, in the lobby, the sheet music and records of the song were stocked in quantity to meet the anticipated demand when the audience left the theater.

Gershwin and his old friend Irving Caesar had discussed writing "Swanee" on a bus ride to upper Manhattan, where the composer now lived, and had written it in half an hour with a poker game going on in the next room. The first person to perform it was Mr. Gershwin, with his favorite comb and tissue paper. Both Gershwin and Caesar were sure that "Swanee" would be a hit too. But with all the unpredictability of show business, audiences left the Capitol Theater neither humming the new song nor stopping to buy it at the music counter in the lobby. Soon it looked as if "Swanee" would take its place in that enormous category—the forgotten song. Caesar was so discouraged that he offered to sell out his rights for two hundred dollars, but Gershwin managed to persuade him not to.

A few months later, Al Jolson, the famous singer whom Gershwin had met during the tryout of *La La Lucille* in Atlantic City, asked the young composer to a party. For Gershwin a party always meant one thing: playing the piano. At Jolson's he did just that, soon slipping into the smooth, catchy tune of "Swanee." Jolson was entranced. What was the name of it? Why hadn't he heard it before? Jolson was performing at a theater directly across Broadway from the Capitol Theater. Would Gershwin let *him* sing "Swanee"?

The whimsical ways of show business are such that when "Swanee" crossed the street and was sung by Al Jolson at the Winter Garden it became the hit of the season, and it was to be one of the most enduring of the Gershwin songs. Within a year a million copies of the sheet music and 2,250,000 phonograph records had been sold and each of the slightly stunned young men had collected ten thousand dollars in royalties.

"There's no business like show business——" Though Irving Berlin actually wrote that famous song, George Gershwin certainly could have set the words to music with equal feeling. Show business suddenly had made him rich and famous. And why? Because his song had gone from the west to the east side of Broadway.

It seemed to most people that Gershwin had now climbed the stairway to success. One person disagreed: Gershwin himself. He had always wanted success and money and now he had them. But he wanted something more, something far more difficult to achieve—to write a great piece of music.

Gershwin's "Swanee" flopped at the Capitol and then became a hit a few months later when Al Jolson sang it at the Winter Garden.

CULVER PICTURES, INC.

5 / Rhapsody in Blue

WITH THE COMING of the twenties, America swept into a dizzy period of forgetfulness and folly. Skirts began to go up; so did the stock market; so did organized crime in the form of bootlegging, thanks to the new law against the manufacture or sale of liquor. A craze for jazz swept the country and gave the era its name.

Pure Dixieland jazz, with musicians improvising in an exhilarating, inspired fashion, could only be heard in the large cities. But its trademarks—"hot" trumpet playing, the "dirty" sound of the blues, the free-swinging, endlessly varied jazz style—were taken up by every band, great and small, famous or otherwise, all over the country. Plump, moon-faced Paul Whiteman, a Colorado-born student of serious music, was so enthusiastic about jazz and so bothered by the fact that many bands "jazzed" one tune well and the next badly that he organized his own band, for which he wrote carefully worked-out arrangements. Soon he became known as the "King of Jazz," with a huge following of fans called cake-eaters.

Young people during this period began to act in what some considered such a wild and reckless manner, rushing about in their roadsters, brandishing hip flasks filled with bootleg alcohol and being so terribly familiar with one another, that jazz was blamed for their behavior. Immoral! Indecent! The music of savages! thundered men of the church and pompous educators about jazz. *The New York Times* solemnly reported that a former cornetist in Queen Victoria's private orchestra had dropped dead the first time he heard American jazz. Jazz was blamed for all the disorders of the human race from drunkenness to suicide.

Jazz was also a worry to composers of serious music and to intellectuals. What attitude should they adopt toward jazz? Certainly it was a new, distinctive kind of music. But was it anything more than a craze—as the jaunty cakewalk had been a craze in the days of the minstrel show? Some dared to believe that in jazz America had at last come up with her own music. Others went further: jazz, they declared, was the *only* music. Symphonic music was as out of date as the Gregorian chant. The arguments raged back and forth.

Though few people realized it at the time, the one composer uniquely equipped to settle the controversy was George Gershwin. By 1922 his name was well known in musical circles. George Gershwin? Of course—that clever composer of Broadway shows, including those yearly editions of George White's *Scandals*. Wasn't he the one who had written that catchy "I'll Build a Stairway to Paradise" and the rooty-toot "Boy Wanted"?

What scarcely anyone could know was that whenever he had the time Gershwin continued to study with Edward Kilenyi, working at more and more complicated exercises in harmony, learning orchestration and how to write for the various instruments. One well-known musician of the day, however, recognized Gershwin's quality just from his Broadway songs. In September, 1922, Beryl Rubinstein, a concert pianist and member of the faculty of the Cleveland Institute of Music, was quoted by the newspapers as saying of Gershwin, "This young fellow has the spark of musical genius which is definite in his serious moods. . . . This young fellow has the fire of originality. . . . With Gershwin's style and seriousness he is not definitely from the popular music school, but one of the really astounding figures in the country's musical efforts. . . . I really believe that America will at no distant date honor [him] for his talent . . . and that when we speak of American composers George Gershwin's name will be prominent on the list."

Meanwhile the controversy continued. That low-down, devilish, sin-making jazz—was it a vulgar passing fancy or was it musically important? European composers like Debussy, Stravinsky and Milhaud thought well enough of *"le jazz hot"* to draw on its rhythms and colors for their compositions, but none of them handled the jazz idiom with the confidence of one to whom it was native music. Such a one was George Gershwin, and in August, 1922, he made his first move toward writing a serious jazz composition.

There is an unfortunate tradition in America to this day: people are slightly suspicious of opera. All that arm-waving and chest-heaving, all those velvet-clad characters with unpronounceable names blundering around fighting duels, going mad and singing about their troubles—usually in a strange language. To many Americans the whole thing seems foreign and ridiculous and pretentious. On the other hand, America has always been enthusiastic about musical plays which have recognizable situations and are sung in English. Many of these "musicals"—take *Most Happy Fella,* for example—are, in fact, full-length American operas—but the producers are careful not to call them by that name lest it frighten away the public.

In 1922, before the days of radio and modern recording

techniques, opera was a good deal less popular than it is today. Imagine the surprise of an audience assembled in a New Haven, Connecticut, theater for the tryout of the latest George White *Scandals* to find that sandwiched in among the star acts, the extravagant production numbers and the usual lineups of gorgeous girls there was to be a one-act jazz opera by George Gershwin. *Opera* in a Broadway revue? It was unheard of. And a tragic opera at that, all about love and jealousy and death.

Gershwin had described his ideas for the opera to George White earlier that summer: the story would take place in Harlem using an all-Negro cast, and the music would be in true jazz style with "hot" and "blues" numbers. But all the dialogue was to be sung in proper operatic fashion and there would be a continuous orchestral accompaniment. Gershwin never thought that the producer would actually consider using a one-act opera in his revue. He was amazed when White, less than a month before the tryout was to open in New Haven, decided that it might be just the kind of novelty that would cause a lot of talk about his new show and told Gershwin to go ahead and write it. A simple plot was concocted by the lyricist B. G. DeSylva and, because of the need for haste, Gershwin took most of the music for the opera from songs that he had already written and put away for future use.

Rehearsals began and Gershwin became increasingly nervous. It had been difficult to find popular singers who had enough musical training to perform his score properly, even with the experienced and enthusiastic Paul Whiteman, conductor for the show, to rehearse them. And what would people say, anyway, about a Broadway songwriter's attempt to go "highbrow"? By the opening night in New Haven tension had brought on indigestion—what he often referred to as his "composer's stomach"—which would recur at such moments of stress for the rest of his life.

Far from reacting against this curious operatic novelty in the midst of the *George White Scandals of 1922,* the opening-night audience in New Haven gave *Blue Monday,* as the work was first called, a tremendous ovation. "This opera will be imitated in a hundred years," cheered a critic the next day. Gershwin's hopes rose. He had long believed that jazz could be the basis for a serious musical composition. Was he now going to prove it?

On the night of August 29, 1922, the *Scandals* opened in New York City and the audience was again enthusiastic. But next day the critics disagreed violently:

First Critic: "The first real American opera . . . a genuinely human plot of American life, set to music in the popular vein, using jazz only at the right moments, the sentimental song, the blues, and, above all, a new and free ragtime recitative."

Second Critic: "It was a little bit of *La Bohème* with the 'Liebestod' of *Tristan* to close, burlesqued almost beyond recognition."

First Critic: "True, there were crudities, but in it we see the first gleam of new American musical art."

Third Critic: "The most dismal, stupid and incredible black-face sketch that has probably ever been perpetrated."

George White had put on *Blue Monday* not to further the cause of American musical art but because he was a good showman and hoped the novelty of it would attract people to his new revue. Now it seemed to him that the tragic ending of the opera was having such a depressing effect on the audience that it could not recover the light-hearted frame of mind needed for the rest of the show. After the single opening night performance in New York, George White abruptly withdrew *Blue Monday* from his *Scandals* and it was not seen again.

Time and revivals of the little opera have shown that for the most part the critics who damned *Blue Monday* were right and for the right reasons. The libretto was very weak, almost a satire of an operatic story, and when it came to composing an opera, Gershwin was only a beginner. As with any other craft, he had to learn it.

But this is not to say that the critic who called *Blue Monday* "The first real American opera" was not right, too. Failure it may have been and of little interest musically to us today, but it is a milestone in the history of American music.

Another year passed. In the spring of 1923 Gershwin went to England to write a musical comedy for the London stage. It was the first time he had gone abroad, and he was utterly charmed when an immigration official at Southampton asked him if he was "*the* George Gershwin, writer of 'Swanee'?" "Couldn't ask for a more pleasant entrance into a country," he wrote to Ira. George liked the English accent, the English tailoring and the traditional English politeness and made many new friends. He found the state of the English theater less impressive. Unused to their theatrical methods and possibly a little homesick for the protective circle of his family, Gershwin turned out a weak score for the musical comedy, which failed to run. He returned to America richer in experience and by fifteen hundred dollars—his fee for the show.

In his absence the virtues and horrors of jazz had continued to be argued back and forth. One of its strongest supporters was Carl Van Vechten, the former music critic turned novelist, who took the keenest interest in the development of

AEOLIAN HALL
34 West 43rd Street

Thursday Evening
NOVEMBER 1st
Nineteen twenty-three
at 8.15 P. M.

RECITAL OF ANCIENT AND MODERN MUSIC FOR VOICE
by
EVA
GAUTHIER

MAX JAFFE, At the Piano.

I

ANCIENT
a. Dolente Immagine (Romanza da) .... Vincenzo Bellini
b. La Lusinga (Arietta da) .... Gio. B. Perucchini
c. When I have often heard ... . } Henry Purcell
d. Hark! Hark! the Echoing Air "The Fairy Queen" .... }
Author of words unknown

II

MODERN HUNGARIAN AND GERMAN
a. Two Folk and Two Modern Hungarian Songs .... Bela Bartok
b. Auf der Treppe sitzen meine Orchen .... } Paul Hindemith
c. Durch die Abendlichen Gärten .... }
Poems by Christian Morgenstern & Herrian Schilling.

III

AMERICAN
a. The Siren's song (P. G. Woodhouse) .... Jerome Kern
b. Everybody step (Irving Berlin) .... Irving Berlin
c. Innocent ingenue baby (Brian Hooker) .... } George Gershwin
d. Stairway to paradise .... }
(words by R. G. De Silva & Arthur Francis)
e. Swanee (I. Caesar) .... George Gershwin
GEORGE GERSHWIN AT THE PIANO.

IV

AUSTRIAN
Lied der Waldtaube (aus "Gurrelieder") .... Arnold Schönberg
(J. B Jacobson)
Pianoforte arrangement by Alban Berg

V

BRITISH
THE BALLADS OF THE FOUR SEASONS
Spring - Summer - Autumn - Winter (New) .... Arthur Bliss
Words by Li-Po

VI

FRENCH
a. Chant de la Nourrice (Poemes Juifs) .... 1916 Darius Milhaud
b. L'Alouette (Du Baras) ...... (New) .... Maurice Delage
c. 2 Chansons Espagnols ...... (New) .... }
d. Sur les murs de Salamanca .... } Swan Hennessy
e. Mon voisin est don Henriques (New) .... }

Tickets 75c., $1.00, $1.50, $2.00. Boxes $15.00 Plus 10% War Tax.
On Sale at Aeolian Hall Box Office.

Management: WOLFSOHN MUSICAL BUREAU, INC.

Victor Records. Steinway Piano Used

Eva Gauthier startled concertgoers by singing a selection of jazz and pop songs as well as classical music at Aeolian Hall in 1923.

IRA GERSHWIN COLLECTION

the arts in America. One night in the fall of 1923, Van Vechten received a telephone call from the famous soprano Eva Gauthier, who told him that on the program of her November recital at Aeolian Hall she was going to include a jazz group.

A recital by Eva Gauthier was an important musical event and would call a lot of attention to jazz being performed on a serious program of music. "She is doing this great service to the American people in no half-hearted way either," Van Vechten wrote excitedly to a journalist friend. "The songs are not to be sandwiched in between opera airs and English ballads. They are immediately preceded on the program by the name of Béla Bartók, and they are followed by Schönberg's *Gurrelieder*. George Gershwin is to play her accompaniments for this group, which will include his splendid 'I'll Build a Stairway to Paradise.' "

George Gershwin, the man who wrote the music for the brassy George White *Scandals,* playing for Eva Gauthier at conservative Aeolian Hall! Whatever next? The excited Van Vechten urged his journalist friend to give as much attention as possible to the concert.

Van Vechten continued, "I consider this one of the very most important events in American musical history and it will lure me back to the concert hall, from which I have held aloof for two years. It is a pleasure to do everything one can for an artist who is perspicacious enough to realize the importance of the only really alive music that is being composed anywhere today. Of course you could hardly complain that this music does not get a hearing and a good hearing, too. (I consider Paul Whiteman's Orchestra about the best in the world, and there are plenty of vaudeville singers who do these tunes justice) but most serious musicians in this country, although willing to sing or play 'The Old Folks at Home' or some early German or French folk song, seem to feel that 'Alexander's Ragtime Band,' 'Ragging the Scale,' 'Waiting for the Robert E. Lee,' 'Swanee,' 'Running Wild' and other such songs, among the indubitable works of genius that this country has produced, are beneath contempt. This is not the opinion of Ravel, or of Stravinsky, or of the Six. One of the most famous of the European moderns wires me impatiently to send him all the new ones.

"I suggest that we get up a torchlight procession headed by Paul Whiteman and his orchestra to honor Miss Gauthier, the pioneer. Mind you, I prophesy that the Philharmonic will be doing it in two years."

And in two years, almost to the day, not the Philharmonic, but its rival, the New York Symphony Society, *was* doing it.

Eva Gauthier's much anticipated recital took place at Aeolian Hall on the evening of November 1, 1923. More than halfway through the program, she appeared with a different accompanist than before—young George Gershwin, who was clutching a small bundle of sheet music with lurid black and yellow covers. He looked pale and tense, and a critic noted that he was "far from possessing the icy aplomb of those to whom playing on the platform of Aeolian Hall is an old story." The most prodigiously talented musician of his day, Gershwin always held in awe serious composers, music critics and intellectuals. Now he had invaded their world and he was nervous.

Eva Gauthier, splendidly dressed in black and diamonds, nodded to him that she was ready to begin, and Gershwin broke into the introduction to 'Alexander's Ragtime Band.' A stir of pleasure ran through the house. There were six songs in the jazz group, including three by Gershwin himself. "The audience," remarked Deems Taylor, critic for the New York *Evening World,* "was just as much fun to watch as the songs were to hear, for it began by being just a trifle patronizing and ended by completely surrendering to the alluring rhythms of our own folk music." A high moment for the musically sophisticated in the hall was when Gershwin slyly worked into the accompaniment of his "I'll Build a Stairway to Paradise" an appropriate quotation from Rimski-Korsakov's *Schéhérazade.* When the group was finished, a storm of applause broke from the audience. It looked as if Lady Jazz (a popular metaphor of the time) had, for the moment, anyway, become a respectable woman in the presence of the musical elite of New York.

"It seemed to one listener," Deems Taylor wrote the following Sunday, summing up his opinion of the concert, "that the six jazz numbers stood up amazingly well, not only as entertainment but as music. Some of them had their vulgar moments—but it is not for a reviewer who hears the *Marche Slav* and the *Fourteenth Rhapsody* a dozen times a season to refer to the subject of vulgarity. . . . What they did possess was melodic interest and continuity, harmonic appropriateness, well balanced, almost classically severe form, and subtle and fascinating rhythms—in short, the qualities that any sincere and interesting music possesses."

The concert was also Gershwin's first important public appearance as a pianist, giving people an opportunity to hear the amazing quality of his playing. When Eva Gauthier repeated the recital with him in Boston, a critic for one of the evening papers was astonished at the way Gershwin improved his accompaniments "with cross-rhythms; wove them into a pliant and changing counterpoint; set in pauses and accents; sustained cadences; gave character to the measures wherein the singer's voice was still." These, of course, are familiar features of jazz playing today; then, they were utterly new and different. European composers "might draw hints and profits" from Gershwin's playing, continued the critic. "In America . . . he is the beginning of sophisticated jazz."

Encouraged by the success of the Gauthier recital the pro-jazz forces pressed on. At their head was the band leader Paul Whiteman, with his tiny moustache, hefty size and passionate belief in jazz. As America's "King of Jazz," Whiteman's realm was extensive. He controlled eleven bands in New York City and seventeen on the road and received royalties from forty more which played his arrangements, many of them written by his clever pianist, Ferde Grofé. Whiteman's resulting income amounted to around a million dollars a year.

"Jazz," Whiteman often declared, "is the music of our time and we are not living in an age of decadence." Having studied as a serious musician, he was eager to prove his claim to other serious musicians. He conceived the idea of hiring Aeolian Hall for "An Experiment in Modern Music" and playing an entire program of jazz songs and arrangements to an invited audience of distinguished musicians. To give the occasion special importance, he planned to commission a number of new jazz works for it.

Whiteman had conducted Gershwin's opera, *Blue Monday*, and greatly admired it. It was natural for him, then, to ask George if he would write a jazz concerto for his projected concert. Gershwin, busy working on a new musical comedy called *Sweet Little Devil*, answered vaguely that he might be interested, but committed himself no further than that—particularly since no date had been set for the concert.

Late in the evening of January 3, 1924, the Gershwin brothers were in one of their favorite haunts, a billiard parlor on Broadway. It was typical of the pair that George should actually be playing the game with the same ferocious energy and intensity that he brought to whatever he did while Ira was seated comfortably against a wall, carefully reading the early morning edition of the New York *Herald*. Suddenly Ira jerked to attention. Tucked away on the amusement page was a small item announcing that Paul Whiteman and his band were going to present "An Experiment in Modern Music at Aeolian Hall." Victor Herbert had agreed to write an original work for it, the report continued, and George Gershwin, a jazz concerto. The concert would take place on the afternoon of February 12.

The next morning George telephoned Whiteman and hotly demanded an explanation. Somebody else had gotten the idea of presenting a jazz program, said the genial conductor, so he had been forced to schedule the concert sooner than he had planned. As for the announcement about the jazz concerto—that was an error. But, Whiteman begged, wouldn't Gershwin consider writing it anyway? Didn't Whiteman realize that February 12 was only a month away? George protested. Think about it, pleaded Whiteman—just think about it.

A jazz concerto. The idea began to take hold of Gershwin's imagination. A jazz concerto. Just the kind of piece he had always wanted to write. But could he do it? There was so little time. On the other hand, he always worked well under pressure . . .

A jazz concerto. He could not shake the idea from his mind. It took turns worrying him, then exciting him. Finally he had an idea. He called Whiteman and said he would be willing to write the work if someone else could orchestrate it. He didn't have the time and, besides, he wasn't sure enough of himself. That would be fine, said Whiteman—he had his own right-hand man, Ferde Grofé, one of the best arrangers in the country.

The next day Gershwin went up to Boston for the opening of *Sweet Little Devil.* Out of the "steely rhythms and rattly bangs" of the train he began to gather ideas for his new composition, forming what he later described as "a definite plot of the piece, as distinguished from its actual substance." Gershwin, at the time, was very much under the spell of one of Liszt's Hungarian rhapsodies, and it was in this loosely connected rhapsody or fantasia form that the work took shape in his mind.

Back in New York on January 7, Gershwin began to compose his rhapsody seated at an upright piano in the back of his family's apartment on 110th Street. The work went well and he soon had most of the lively first section sketched out; what was needed now was a slow theme, something warm and moving and full of melodic sweep. A night or two later he went to a party and took his usual place at the piano. A party simply wasn't a party to George unless he was at the piano, playing his own and everyone else's old songs or improvising new ones. Suddenly his fingers moved into a broad, almost hymnlike melody that simply came mysteriously from somewhere inside him—the theme he had been looking for. George was sure of it. So was Ira.

As work on the piece continued, Ira, always interested in literary matters, wanted to know what George was going to call it. George pointed out that since in technical musical language the piece was a rhapsody, he had thought of naming it American Rhapsody. Ira was unimpressed. It happened that he had just been to an exhibition of paintings by Whistler which bore such names as "Harmony in Grey and Green" and "Nocturne in Blue and Green." Why not call the new work Rhapsody in Blue? Ira suggested impulsively, and the most popular piece of concert music ever written by an American composer had a name.

February 12 loomed closer, and Gershwin worked frantically to complete his two-piano version of the rhapsody, handing it sheet by sheet to Ferde Grofé for orchestration. Careful workman that Gershwin was, he kept revising the score, making small changes in detail here and there, struggling always to make it better. The fully orchestrated rhapsody was not given to Whiteman until one week before the concert.

Wildly enthusiastic about it, Whiteman promptly invited a number of musicians and critics to a rehearsal. Among them was Victor Herbert, who made a valuable suggestion as to how to make the beautiful slow theme sound even more effective. Some of the critics liked the work as much as Whiteman; others were more doubtful. One scratched his head and said, "Who's Gershwin?"

The day of the concert arrived. Among the great musicians of the time that Whiteman had invited were violinists Fritz Kreisler and Jascha Heifetz, conductors Walter Damrosch and Leopold Stokowski and composers Rachmaninoff and Stravinsky—and of course he invited all the music critics. He had added nine extra players to his band and published an elaborately decorated program. Even with every seat in the house occupied, Whiteman would lose seven thousand dollars on the afternoon.

Suddenly the enormity of what he was about to do overwhelmed him. While Gershwin remained, for once, strangely

Paul Whiteman and his orchestra presented "An Experiment in Modern Music" at Aeolian Hall on February 12, 1924. CULVER PICTURES, INC.

calm, his "composer's stomach" in some kind of order, Whiteman lost his nerve. How had he dared to ask the greatest musicians of the day—artists for whom he had the most profound respect—to come and listen to a program of cheap jazz arrangements? What had he been thinking of?

On the way to Aeolian Hall, Whiteman was sure that he was sick, even dying. Once there, in a torrent of nervousness, he paced the backstage area, then finding the atmosphere stifling, went out to see what was happening at the entrance to the auditorium. There he beheld a terrifying sight. "It was snowing," as he recalled later, "but men and women were fighting to get into the door, pulling and mauling each other as they sometimes do at a baseball game, or a prize fight, or in the subway. Such was my state of mind by this time that I wondered if I had come to the right entrance. And then I saw Victor Herbert going in. It was the right entrance, sure enough, and the next day the ticket office people said they could have sold out the house ten times over."

The audience that had gathered appeared to Whiteman to be a very strange one indeed. "Vaudevillians, concert managers come to have a look at the novelty, Tin Pan Alleyites, composers, symphony and opera stars, flappers, cake-eaters," all mixed up together.

"I went backstage again, more scared than ever," Whiteman continues in his reminiscences. "Black fear simply possessed me. I paced the floor, gnawed my thumbs and vowed I'd give five thousand dollars if we could stop right then and there. Now that the audience had come perhaps I really had nothing to offer them at all. I even made excuses to keep the curtain from rising on schedule. But finally there was no longer any way of postponing the evil moment. The curtain went up and before I could dash forth, as I was tempted to do, and announce that there wouldn't be any concert we were in the midst of it."

The program was a very long one, some twenty-odd selections in all, with the *Rhapsody in Blue* placed second to the end. There were three "semisymphonic arrangements" of Irving Berlin songs, jazz versions of Edward MacDowell's "To a Wild Rose" and Rudolf Friml's "Chansonette," and the world premiere of Victor Herbert's composition called "A Suite of Serenades." As the afternoon wore away, the audience became bored, then frankly restless. There was little contrast to the selections; most of them sounded pretty much the same. As for Victor Herbert's new work, he might be a fine composer of operettas, but when it came to writing for a jazz band he wasn't up to much. Despite the number of flappers and cake-eaters present who worshipped Paul Whiteman, the applause was mild, the enthusiasm nonexistent. The conductor's worst fears seemed to be coming true.

By the time he finally reached the *Rhapsody in Blue,* Whiteman was in despair. Gershwin appeared onstage, took his place at the piano and, having made the necessary adjustments to his chair, nodded to the conductor that he was ready to begin. With a feeling of almost hopelessness, Whiteman threw an opening cue to Ross Gorman, the band's brilliant clarinet player. Gorman lifted his instrument and let out the famous, slowly ascending wail which begins the *Rhapsody*. Higher and higher up the scale rose the clarinet—seventeen dizzy notes stretching the tension and gathering the astonished attention of the audience. The score had been written so hastily that there were blank places in which Gershwin simply improvised, but the performance went brilliantly. In the hall the excitement began to mount and Whiteman felt it. "Somewhere in the middle of the score I began crying," he recalled later. "When I came to myself I was eleven pages along and to this day I cannot tell you how I conducted that far." The final brash, exhilarating notes died away and the audience rose to its feet and gave the *Rhapsody* a wild ovation.

Audiences have been rising to their feet and cheering it ever since.

The *Rhapsody in Blue* is probably Gershwin's best-loved piece and seems likely to remain so. It is also far and away the most frequently performed piece of concert music by an American composer. Every conceivable kind of transcription has been made of the *Rhapsody*: there is a version for eight pianos and for solo harmonica and even one for violin and orchestra. Ballets in Grecian and modern styles have been danced to it. Condensed and complete performances have been presented in stage shows and in the movies. The name, *Rhapsody in Blue,* was given to the improbable film biography of George Gershwin made in 1946. Within ten years of its composition the *Rhapsody* earned a quarter of a million dollars from the sale of records, sheet music and royalties. The *Rhapsody* made Gershwin a rich man, as well as America's most famous composer.

Musicians have often tried to analyze the secret of the *Rhapsody*'s popularity. Technically the work is crude. Certain connecting passages are diffuse and don't seem to lead anywhere, as if Gershwin couldn't think what to do next. Of the two sections, the first is half again as long as the second, making the piece top-heavy; and in both parts, musicians have detected borrowings in style and color from Chopin, Debussy, Liszt, Tchaikovsky and even Oriental music. Finally, there is the charge that the *Rhapsody* cannot be taken as a serious piece of music because it was not orchestrated by the composer himself.

These faults may all exist, but the simple fact is that the vitality, drama and sentiment of the *Rhapsody* override them all. Whatever influences went into the piece, it came out American: American in its nervous rhythms, its gaiety, its blues mood—its heart. And as for the charge that another man did the orchestration, it can be answered that Ferde Grofé performed his work in a masterly fashion, which he himself never bettered, and which has set a style for jazz orchestration ever since.

Though the audience had acclaimed the *Rhapsody in Blue* at its first performance, what did the learned critics—those men whom Gershwin always pretended to ignore and never quite could—have to say about it?

FIRST CRITIC: "This composition shows extraordinary talent, just as it also shows a young composer . . . struggling with a form of which he is far from being master."

SECOND CRITIC: "How trite and feeble and conventional the tunes are."

THIRD CRITIC: "A highly ingenious work."

SECOND CRITIC: ". . . how sentimental and vapid the harmonic treatment."

FOURTH CRITIC: "The beginning and ending of it were stunning. . . ."

FIFTH CRITIC: "It runs off into empty passage work and meaningless repetition."

FOURTH CRITIC: ". . . the beginning, particularly, with a fluttering tongued drunken whoop of an introduction which had the audience rocking."

SIXTH CRITIC: "It was crude, but it hinted at something

new, something that has not hitherto been said in music."

SECOND CRITIC: ". . . weep over the lifelessness of its melody and harmony, so derivative, so static, so inexpressive."

SIXTH CRITIC: "Mr. Gershwin will bear watching; he may yet bring jazz out of the kitchen."

He was famous. He was rich. He was not yet twenty-six years old, but his talent had been recognized by the world. It was a dangerous moment for George Gershwin. Somewhere within himself he knew that he possessed the talent to write a truly great piece of music. The *Rhapsody* was only a beginning—a delightful, lovable composition—but only a beginning. Now he must develop and deepen and seek out new challenges. Standing in the way of this development was his facility—the ease with which he could turn out a new tune and earn a lot of money for it—his need to be the center of attention and the superficiality of the times in which he lived.

6/ Concerto in F

It was 1924—the year that women began to cut their hair short and wear dresses that showed their knees, the year that the funny, frantic new dance, The Charleston, became all the rage. In New York and London people were entertainment mad. The jazz era gathered momentum, and out of it emerged two enchanted figures: F. Scott Fitzgerald, to write the story, and George Gershwin, the music.

New York—January, 1924: *Sweet Little Devil,* music by George Gershwin. . . . New York—Febraury, 1924: at Aeolian Hall, *Rhapsody in Blue* by George Gershwin, the composer at the piano. . . . London—April, 1924: *Primrose,* music by George Gershwin, lyrics by Ira Gershwin. . . . New York—June, 1924: *George White's Scandals of 1924,* music by George Gershwin. . . . London—August, 1924: *Stop Flirting,* interpolated songs by George Gershwin.

Each Gershwin musical seemed to improve on the last. He had failed in England before, but *Primrose* was a huge success. Londoners particularly liked the songs with special British references, such as "Berkeley and Kew" or "Isn't It Terrible What They Did to Mary Queen of Scots?" By 1924, Ira had written the lyrics for several Broadway shows with other composers. In London, having worked on *Primrose* with George, he decided that he had enough of a reputation to call himself by his real name. But poor Ira seemed doomed never to achieve his own identity. The English newspapers, unused to the name Ira (short for Isadore), commented on the novelty of a "brother-sister" song-writing team.

By the summer of 1924 all America was singing George's wistful

> "Somebody loves me I wonder who,
> I wonder who she can be."

from the *Scandals of 1924*. It had what people began to recognize as the Gershwin touch. No one else could have written it.

What would this versatile, wonderfully talented young man do next? As autumn approached, some dared to hope for a new serious jazz composition. Instead, his erstwhile producer, Alex Aarons, interested Gershwin in doing another musical comedy, to star Fred Astaire and his charming sister Adele.

Any musical that had the Astaires in it was up against certain problems, Aarons explained to George. Because the public knew that they were brother and sister they could not play romantic leads. Aarons had in mind some kind of plot in which a young brother and sister get each other in and out of various romantic escapades but end up making appropriate marriages by the final curtain. He had a pair of writers fixing something up along these lines. Meanwhile, he remembered hearing George play a most unusual tune in London the previous spring. It was full of shifting, misplaced accents. If Ira would set some words to it, Aarons wanted to fit it into the show somewhere. The title of the new musical? He was thinking of calling it *Black-Eyed Susan,* but maybe they could come up with something better. Naturally, the name needn't have anything to do with the plot of the show or the characters in it—just as long as it was catchy.

That's how a typical musical comedy of the twenties was put together (and Alex Aarons prided himself that his were more "sophisticated" than most). The plot never mattered except to serve as a peg for the necessary gags, love songs and particular specialties of the stars. Songs were put in and yanked out or switched from one spot to another. It didn't make much difference where they occurred, as long as they stood out effectively; they weren't expected to move the plot forward or reveal character.

George accepted Aaron's commission and, with Ira to do the lyrics, settled down to work. Soon the brothers produced a charming song called "Lady Be Good," which everyone agreed was a much more fetching title for the show than *Black-Eyed Susan. Lady Be Good* it became. Ira also had been sweating over the words of the off-beat tune that Aarons had liked so much. Its syncopated, misplaced accents kept putting Ira off, and he and George had gotten into an argument over which of the last two notes of the refrain should be stressed in the lyric. Finally Ira came up with something that satisfied the brothers' exacting standard, that also seemed to work out as a good idea for a dance routine by the Astaires:

"Fascinating Rhythm
You've got me on the go!
Fascinating Rhythm
I'm all a-quiver."

The show went into rehearsal, and Fred Astaire, stumped for a bang-up ending to one of his dance routines, was amazed when George not only offered a suggestion but proceeded

Fred Astaire, surrounded by befeathered chorus girls, in a number from *Lady Be Good*. CULVER PICTURES, INC.

to get up on the stage and demonstrate it. Seeing George dance with all the bursting vitality and energy that was in his music made Astaire laugh with delight. And the idea was such a good one that he promptly adopted it.

Great enthusiasm greeted *Lady Be Good* when it opened first in Philadelphia. No one seemed to mind the foolishness of the plot. The audience laughed in all the places that they were meant to and clapped for the songs of the Gershwins and the dances of the Astaires. Among the numbers that the critics chose to praise the next day in the newspapers was a poignant ballad sung in Act One by Adele Astaire:

> "Some day he'll come along,
> The man I love;
> And he'll be big and strong,
> The man I love;"

After a week, however, the producers decided that though the song was nice enough and Adele Astaire sang it well, it didn't seem to belong in that particular spot. It slowed down the action. Nor was there a suitable place for it anywhere else. So the song was removed and given back to Gershwin to be used, it was supposed, in some future musical comedy.

Minus "The Man I Love," *Lady Be Good* traveled to New York and turned out to be Gershwin's biggest hit up to that time. "Brisk, inventive, gay, nervous, delightful," wrote one critic about the score, and another said of the Astaires, "The young couple appeared about 8:30 o'clock and from an audience sophisticated and over-theatered received a cordial greeting. At 8:45 they were applauded enthusiastically and when at 9:15 they sang and danced "Fascinating Rhythm" the callous Broadwayites cheered them as if their favorite halfback had planted the ball behind the goal posts after an 80-yard run."

Gershwin was now more than ever the musical man of the hour--the Pied Piper of the jazz age. He was young, attractive and disarmingly self-confident; his company was sought by rich hostesses, beautiful women and the greats of the theater and music worlds. Such adulation could easily have had a disastrous effect on his character had he not gone on living within the protective circle of his family. George might be famous, but they were there to remind him with their warm, no-pretensions-allowed humor that to them he was still *their* George, the tough roller-skating champion of Forsyth Street, the boy who everyone thought was going to turn out to be a vagabond.

It wasn't that they weren't proud of him. "You can't arrest me, officer. I'm the father of George Gershwin," Mr. Gershwin once shouted at a policeman who had stopped him for speeding. Mr. Gershwin spoke with such a strong Jewish accent that the name sounded like "Judge Goishvin." The cop had never heard of Judge Goishvin but assumed that he must be an important man in the city government and let Mr. Gershwin go. Mr. Gershwin's judgments were all his own. He once said proudly of the *Rhapsody in Blue*, "Of course it's a good piece. Doesn't it take fifteen minutes to play?" Not that he was totally unmusical. Many of George's tunes he could recall easily, but not always Ira's lyrics. To Mr. Gershwin "Fascinating Rhythm" was frequently "Fashion on the River."

Mrs. Gershwin was proud too. She had always been ambitious for her sons, though it continued to amaze her that someone could become so successful by writing music. It worried her, too, that half the time George's stomach wouldn't let him eat the big, delicious meals she served up for the family. And to complete the family circle there was younger brother, Arthur, who hoped to be a songwriter too, and the "baby," pretty Frances—or "Frankie" as she was called—who had a small, husky voice and was developing a nice way with a Gershwin song.

With so many members of the family all having so many friends in and out of the apartment on 110th Street, George found it hard to obtain privacy in which to compose. After *Lady Be Good* turned out to be such a hit, the Gershwin family decided to buy a house on 103rd Street near the Hudson River. S. N. Behrman once wrote what a visit to that house was like in *The New Yorker* magazine:

> I hadn't seen the Gershwins in a long time and I telephoned to ask if it would be convenient for me to call. It was a sweltering night in September and I arrived at the house about nine o'clock. For a long time I rang the doorbell but got no answer. Through the screened, curtained door-window I could see figures moving inside and I kept ringing impatiently. Finally I pushed the door open and walked in. Three or four young men I had never seen before were sitting around smoking. Off the hall was a small reception room which had been converted into a billiard room. I peered in—there was a game in progress but I knew none of the players. I asked for George, or his brother, Ira. No one bothered to reply, but one of the young men made a terse gesture in the direction of the upper stories. I went up one flight and there I found a new group. One of them I vaguely recognized from 110th Street and I asked him where George and Ira were. He said he thought they were upstairs. On the third floor I found Arthur, the youngest brother, who had just come in and didn't know who was in the house, but on the fourth I got an answer to my—by this time agonized—cry. I

heard Ira's voice inviting me up to the fifth. I found him . . . trying to keep cool in George's study. "Who under the sun," I asked, "are those fellows playing billiards on the first floor?"

Ira looked almost guilty. "To tell you the truth," he said, "I don't know."

"But you must," I insisted. "They look perfectly at home."

"I really don't," he said. "There's a bunch of fellows from down the street who've taken to dropping in here every night for a game. I think they're friends of Arthur's. But I don't know who they are."

"Where," I demanded sternly, "is George?"

"He's taken his old rooms in the hotel around the corner. He says he's got to have a little privacy." [1]

Poor George. Even the hotel room wasn't always safe, and sometimes members of his family or friends would invade that refuge. Most of his composing, however, was done at the piano of his fifth-floor study. Surrounded by books, souvenirs and portraits of his favorite composers, he would often work late into the night in a screen of smoke from the ever-present cigar in his mouth. Sometimes Mr. Gershwin would sit outside the closed door, listening with a pleased expression when George's playing continued without interruption, looking more worried if it began to falter—and in a panic when it stopped altogether. Once, after a five-minute silence, Mr. Gershwin could bear it no longer. Slipping into the study, he whistled the last theme that Gershwin had played, "Does that help you, George?" he asked.

As Gershwin became increasingly famous, more and more visitors came to the study on the top floor of the 103rd Street house—friends, musicians, famous composers who wanted to

[1] Reprinted by permission from the article "Troubadour" by S. N. Behrman; copyright © 1929, 1957 The New Yorker Magazine, Inc.

meet him, unknown composers looking for help, lyricists with lines they wanted him to set to music, newspaper interviewers, autograph seekers. The list was varied—and endless. With his own struggles fresh in his memory, Gershwin always found time for them all, whether it was to offer a friendly criticism of someone's favorite song, help launch a promising composer on Broadway or give an interview to a trembling would-be journalist for his high-school newspaper. Smiling and affable, he easily made people feel comfortable with him. A joke often helped break the tension.

Nervous interviewer: "Didn't you play anything when you were a boy?"

Gershwin: "Only hooky."

And of course there was the piano. He was always willing to play for anyone who asked—in fact, more then willing. "I'd bet on George any time—in a hundred-yard dash to the piano," his sardonic friend Oscar Levant once remarked.

Of the many musicians who came to see him, Gershwin could usually assume that they wanted something—advice, encouragement, perhaps even money. Early in 1925, however, Gershwin received a distinguished caller with a different kind of request. This was Walter Damrosch, the gruff-looking conductor of the New York Symphony Society, who had done much to further the cause of good music in America and good American music. Present at Aeolian Hall for the famous first performance of the *Rhapsody in Blue*, Damrosch had been greatly impressed by Gershwin's talents and was now prepared to commission him to write a piano concerto. With the composer as soloist, Damrosch would like to perform it at seven concerts in four cities: New York, Washington, Baltimore and Philadelphia.

A piano concerto!—that most difficult to write, most beautiful form of music. Beethoven had written five, Brahms two. Schumann and Grieg had been content with one successful attempt each. Some great composers had never dared to try. Was he, a mere beginner, up to it? Gershwin asked himself. It would require time, deeper study of the concerto form. Naturally, too, he would have to do the orchestration. Then there was the fee to consider. The New York Symphony Society could not afford to pay nearly as much as he could earn from a Broadway show. But to write a piano concerto was a challenge—a challenge to compose a great piece of music. Gershwin accepted it.

Excitedly, he set to work under the usual conditions at 103rd Street. S. N. Behrman remembers seeing George at work on the score of the concerto "in a room where there must have been six other people, talking among themselves, having tea and playing checkers." Improvising a new tune for a song under such conditions might be perfectly all right, but even the ever-sociable George saw that this was no way to write a piano concerto.

The well-known musician Ernest Hutcheson was offering a course in advanced piano at Chautauqua, New York, and, hearing of Gershwin's need for a quiet place to work, made available an empty studio to him. It proved to be the first of only two times that George ever left the attentive company of his family and friends and the opportunity to go to parties in order to concentrate deeply and in solitude on a piece of music that he was writing.

At Chautauqua, the students were so excited at having the brilliant pianist-composer in their midst that they hung about his studio waiting for a chance to hear him play. Hutcheson finally had to make a rule that no one was to go into the vicinity of the building until four o'clock in the afternoon.

George Gershwin and Ernest Hutcheson at Chautauqua in July, 1925.
CULVER PICTURES, INC.

In the meantime, Gershwin had received offers to do not one but two Broadway shows: the first, a pseudo-Russian operetta, the other, a sophisticated musical comedy. With that daring which was so much a part of George's makeup—there is a Yiddish word, *chutzpa*, that describes it even more accurately—he agreed to write the scores for both of these shows as well as compose the concerto.

Work on the concerto began in July, 1925, and was finished by late September. Orchestrating it took another five weeks, and not until November 10 did he finally mark the score "completed." The fact that this was his first attempt at scoring worried him, and since he was a wealthy man, he was able to hire sixty musicians for an afternoon to play through the concerto, with his great friend William Daly conducting, in order to hear how it sounded. About the same time, both musicals went into rehearsal.

So it happened that everything came to a head in December of 1924. Damrosch scheduled the world premiere of the Concerto in F at Carnegie Hall on the afternoon of December 3, with a repeat performance the following day. Gershwin would then play five additional out-of-town performances. The sophisticated musical comedy *Tip Toes* was scheduled to open on December 28 and the operetta *The Song of the Flame,* on the 30th of the month. Both, naturally, would require changes and supervision by the composer before their premieres. As if that weren't enough, Paul Whiteman desired to hire Carnegie Hall on practically the only free night left to Gershwin, December 29, and give a concert version of the one-act opera *Blue Monday*. Rechristened *135th Street,* it had a new orchestration by Ferde Grofé. Gershwin would, of course, have to look in on rehearsals of that.

Was there any limit to the man's energy?

It had snowed for the premiere of the *Rhapsody in Blue;* rain fell on the day of the first performance of the concerto. But the same old mixture of serious musicians, old vaudevillians, intellectuals and popular entertainers turned out as before. The program included a seldom-played symphony by Glazunov; the concerto made up the second half.

As the concert progressed Gershwin became more and more tense. It was a far more difficult moment for him than the premiere of the *Rhapsody.* Here he was, a popular songwriter, daring to invade New York's most important concert hall and join the company of the greatest composers and best pianists of all time. By their standards would he be judged.

Buzzers warned of the end of the intermission, and the expectant audience returned to their seats in the old auditorium, with its dark red walls. A moment later Gershwin walked out onto the stage, accompanied by Walter Damrosch, and seated himself at the piano. "I prophesy that the Philharmonic will be doing it in two years," Carl Van Vechten had said, referring to the playing of works by jazz composers. Two years had passed, almost to the day.

The Concerto in F is in the standard three-movement form and is scored for modern symphony orchestra plus xylophone, bells and hats for the trumpets to play into in the blues section. It has a strange, arresting beginning: the kettledrum pounds, the orchestra gives a shriek, the cymbals clash. A nervous, hectic mood pervades the first movement, reminiscent of the slightly desperate gaiety that was so characteristic of the era in which Gershwin lived.

With the second movement the music deepens. The sense of a specific period in time drops away; it is no time and all time. Robert Payne has written affectingly of this most affecting movement, "It is all poetry. . . . There is a shimmering gaiety, a quietness, a sense of worlds unfolding." The third movement returns to a world more feverish than ever, breathless, frantic, shallow—but enormously exciting.

Throughout the concerto there is such an endless flow of invention, variation and effective scoring that we can hardly believe it was Gershwin's first serious orchestral composition in a classic form. The audience was astonished and impressed and moved, and when the work was over rose to its feet and cheered this extraordinary young musician who appeared to be equally at home in Carnegie Hall or on the Great White Way. Not so the critics, many of whom condemned the concerto:

First Critic: "Conventional . . ."

Second Critic: "Fragmentary . . ."

First Critic: "Trite . . ."

Second Critic: "Uncertain in form . . ."

Third Critic: "He alone . . . expresses us."

Fourth Critic: "It is interesting and individual."

First Critic: "At its worst a little dull . . ."

Fifth Critic: "Much less interesting than the *Rhapsody in Blue* . . ."

Gershwin scarcely had time to heed what the critics said—and anyway, he always pretended not to pay any attention to them. Yet how ironic it was that when his sophisticated comedy *Tip Toes* opened on December 28, there was an explosion of praise for his score—"so fresh and unstinted, the gay young blood of his invention." To top it all, the next evening Gershwin, attempting to be serious, failed again at Carnegie Hall. "An unimpressive accompaniment for an old hokum vaudeville skit," was what one critic said of the new version of his opera, *Blue Monday*.

Today, of course, Gershwin's Concerto in F is a much-played, much-loved work. Yet one wonders whether, after the premiere, Gershwin may not have asked himself if it was worth struggling to become a serious composer, when his efforts were so disdainfully rejected by people whose opinions he could not help but value. Why not go on instead with Broadway, turning out tunes that mirrored people's moods and touched their hearts—tunes that sang the spirit of the times? Wasn't this a more important contribution than writing a concerto and an opera that the experts said were failures?

Whether he came to any conscious decision we do not know, but with the coming of 1926 Gershwin plunged back into the world of Broadway, of gaiety, and again became the center of attention at parties. He was to write attractive "party" compositions for symphony orchestra in the years that followed. But the great piece of music that he had once dreamed of writing seemed to have died before it was ever born.

7 / An American in Paris

IN SOME RESPECTS there is a certain parallel between the careers of Wolfgang Amadeus Mozart and George Gershwin. Both were prodigies, though Mozart was the more fortunate in having a musical father who exposed his son in infancy to music and gave him a thorough musical training. In comparison Gershwin's self-teaching seems all the more remarkable. Yet both composers at an early age, simply laid their hands on a keyboard and found that in some mysterious way these hands, like those of a puppet, obeyed unquestioningly the musical ideas in their heads.

This gift was what made both men such remarkable pianists. Once, when playing in Naples, Mozart had to take off a ring that he was wearing to prove to the superstitious Neapolitans that it had no power, as they believed, to make him perform so magically. The great conductor Serge Koussevitzky heard Gershwin play and wrote afterward, "As I watched him, I caught myself thinking in a dream state that this was a delusion, the enchantment of this extraordinary being too great to be real."

Another musician, Dimitri Tiomkin, said of Gershwin's playing, "Though lacking method and technique, his hands seemed to blend with the keyboard, as if his fingers had an organic unity with the keys and the music flowed from them. His whole body moved with his hands and the music, swaying, bending, twisting. There was no suggestion of exhibitionism or showmanship. Rather, you were reminded of some blithesome person who seems to dance as he walks. It was musical magic, George Gershwin playing Gershwin."

Nor does the parallel between Gershwin and Mozart end here. Both composers had the most extraordinary facility: their minds were like vast warehouses stored with bales and bales of music waiting to be taken out and used. A rare and wonderful gift this facility—but it was also a handicap. The two composers were able to please almost too easily.

Desperately in need of a rich patron who would give him an income to live on while he composed, Mozart went all over Europe selling his talent, so to speak, by composing in the Italian style in Italy, in the French manner in France and so forth. Whatever was ordered—church music, dance music, an aria for a soprano to show off her voice, a pretty serenade—Mozart could easily provide works that were utterly charming and pleasing and appropriate. Mozart never found a patron. In the days when he composed, no copyright protected his works. He was paid only for the first performance of a composition; there were no fat royalties to flow in afterward. Gradually, poverty engulfed him and the struggle began to exhaust his health. Yet the music of these grim years was his deepest and most beautiful. He composed not so much to please others as to satisfy some inner desire of his own, and, succeeding, gave the world a pleasure it had never conceived of before.

Gershwin, with his incredible facility and handicap of lack of musical training, also set about to please the world—and did. Here the parallel with Mozart does not continue. Gershwin's world was a twentieth-century one, and in giving musical pleasure Gershwin quickly swirled up to staggering heights of fame and wealth. From a comparatively early period there was no struggle—only the continuing sense of astonishment that he, a boy who had grown up in poor surroundings, the son of immigrant parents who spoke poor English, could with such ease become the center of worldwide attention and the recipient of enormous wealth. "I'm the happiest man in the world," he once said to Dimitri Tiomkin. "I get paid so much for what I want to do most of all."

There is a poem by the famous German poet Heine which begins: "*Aus meinen grossen Schmerzen mach ich die kleinen Lieder* . . . ("Out of my great sorrows I write my little songs . . .") It is a curious logic which says that an artist must have an understanding of suffering and even despair in order to create a work that, by its beauty and depth of feeling, has the power to take people from despair. Yet again and again, careful study of the lives of painters, musicians and writers, as well as performing artists, has shown that this is so.

A group of Gershwin's friends and admirers once presented him with a brass humidor engraved with their signatures. A wise and elderly spokesman for the group, Otto H. Kahn, made a little speech to him: "I believe in you with full faith and admiration, in your personality, your gifts, in your art, in your future, in your significance in the field of American music. . . . And just because of that I could wish for you an experience—not too prolonged—of that driving storm and stress of the emotions, of that solitary wrestling with your own soul, of that aloofness . . . which are the most effective ingredients for the deepening and mellowing . . . of an artist's inner being and spiritual powers."

However, there is one other parallel between the lives of Mozart and Gershwin. Mozart died when he was thirty-five and some have attributed his incredible facility and energy to his sensing that he had less time than most men to accomplish what he wanted to do in life.

Gershwin had exactly the same kind of vitality, joined with unbelievable musical facility. Could he have sensed in some strange way that he would die at the age of thirty-eight?

It is hard to believe that Gershwin had any such premonition in 1926 or the years that followed. Except for his "composer's stomach," his health was excellent, his energy nothing short of awesome. He drank moderately, was a night owl but slept all morning, took sensible care of himself and seemed to have few, if any, inner problems. His life was carefree, and never more so than in that year of 1926.

Early in the spring, he had knocked out a fast-moving tune for a new musical that was coming up in the fall called *Oh Kay*. Both he and Ira had about decided to use it for a brisk dance number, when George, who never stopped worrying about his compositions until he felt that they were right, inexplicably halved the tempo. Both men realized at once that what they had now was a very beautiful melody for a ballad. Ira Gershwin set to work to write the words, and what came out is indicative of what was on his mind:

> "There's a somebody I'm longing to see:
> I hope that she
> Turns out to be
> Someone who'll watch over me . . ."

That September, Ira married the charming Leonore Strunsky, whose family had always been great friends of the Gershwins. George, as the saying goes, far from losing a brother, gained a sister. Leonore Gershwin moved in with

Ira on the fourth floor of 103rd Street and the three of them remained inseparable for the rest of George's life.

Ira's marriage, however, had raised an interesting question. When was George going to take the big step? After all, he was twenty-seven now—he was getting on. He always had plenty of women around, beautiful women at that. He seemed to attract them as easily as he could write a song. "There was something absolutely charming about him," recalls the lovely dancer and actress Tilly Losch. "He was very full of himself—very sure that the whole world must be interested in George Gershwin. But it was an innocent kind of egotism. You couldn't help liking him even more for it."

Women came and went in George's life and those of his friends who watched the parade would often start matchmaking. Just as soon as they did, George would fool them. This woman was older than he was, he would explain; that one came from Park Avenue and their respective worlds could never meet. As for *that* girl, he knew he couldn't live with her for the rest of his life after having heard her play some of his music on the piano. Completely absorbed in his career, in making music and playing it, George couldn't seem to give his attention to a permanent relationship. Perhaps the best illustration of his attitude is the story told of him at a party, where he was having a pleasant time with a pretty girl who was sitting on his lap. Dreams of becoming Mrs. Gershwin began to waft through the girl's mind when someone asked George to play. The next thing she knew she was picking herself up off the floor. George was still young, most people thought, and one day he would settle down to marriage and responsibility. Meanwhile, his close relationship with Ira and Leonore gave warmth and intimacy to his life.

Soon after Ira's wedding, the new musical *Oh Kay* went to

Philadelphia for tryouts, and on the third night of the run there occurred another of those ludicrous stage mix-ups that occasionally bedeviled Gershwin's career. P. G. Wodehouse and Guy Bolton, who wrote the book for *Oh Kay*, have described what happened in their amusing book of reminiscences, *Bring On the Girls.*

The hero and heroine had just embarked on their important love scene and, as the authors put it, "a more unfortunate moment for a dog to select for making his appearance on the stage could hardly have been thought of. Long windows stood half open on a moonlit beach; the door to the library was unclosed; there was also a stair. None of these appealed to the canine visitor. He preferred instead to come through the fireplace, where a log fire was flickering realistically. He paid no attention to the footlights and stared at the audience from under shaggy brows like a Scotch elder rebuking sin from the pulpit.

"He then walked over to the proscenium arch, cocked his leg, then scuffled with his feet and made his exit—through the fireplace."

Somehow the two lovers managed to stumble through the ripples of laughter to their duet:

> "I remember the bliss
> Of that wonderful kiss. . . .
> Oh how I'd adore it
> If you would encore it,"

they sang.

"The dog made a second appearance, pausing this time while still in the fireplace, his paws resting on the log as he glanced archly from side to side of the room. He jumped the log and came in wagging his tail."

"Oh do, do, do, what you done,
done, done before, baby,"

continued the hero and heroine frantically. But it was no use. "The storm of laughter drowned the orchestra, and, when the wretched animal, as if in response to repeated admonitions made his way again to the proscenium arch, there was no continuing with the number." [1]

Oh Kay, minus the dog, went on to New York and opened to what was becoming a fairly common reaction to a Gershwin musical—raves. The score was "a marvel," wrote one critic. "Hell, it's almost perfect," exclaimed another. Several songs from *Oh Kay* are still favorites—the lovers' "Do, Do, Do" (which George wrote in a single sitting at the piano) and the appealing "Someone to Watch Over Me."

Gershwin composed no large-scale works for the concert hall that year, but in December he appeared in a recital with another concert singer, the beautiful mezzo-soprano Marguerite D'Alvarez. The old battles over jazz had continued to rage, and Madame D'Alvarez was one of its staunchest defenders. When a clergyman denounced jazz as "music of the savage, intellectual and spiritual debauchery, utter degradation," she snapped back, "Nonsense! When I die I want Gershwin's Concerto in F played over my grave." For her recital she asked Gershwin not only to accompany her in some of his own songs but to appear as a soloist in his own right. George decided to play a transcription of the *Rhapsody* for solo piano and to introduce five of the preludes that he had composed over the past two years.

A hundred years before, the prelude form had been perfected by Chopin, and Gershwin's short, evocative pieces owe

[1] Reprinted by permission of Scott Meredith from *Bring On the Girls* by P. G. Wodehouse and Guy Bolton.

a lot to him. Nevertheless, they stand on their own as original compositions in the unique Gershwin jazz idiom. The Second Prelude, in particular, with its slow, steady, walking figure in the bass and syncopated melody for the right hand is one of the most haunting pieces of music Gershwin ever wrote.

The concert was such a success that the two artists went on tour to Buffalo and Boston. Three of the five preludes that Gershwin played at those recitals were published, and they are much performed today, not only by pianists but in transcription by violinists and whole orchestras.

Gershwin's output of serious music had been small in 1926. The following year there was none at all. Had he lost confidence in himself as a serious composer? Friends who knew music and believed in Gershwin, such as the composers Irving Berlin and Vernon Duke, the clever pianist Oscar Levant and the music critic Samuel Chotzinoff, found it hard to believe.

Then, was it simply the times? Everyone said that Gershwin's music—brash, restless, sometimes sad, though never deeply so—was the perfect expression of the age in which it was written. And by 1927 the pace of that age had become more frantic than ever. As the country sailed merrily before a brisk wind of prosperity that was soon to make a treacherous shift, skirts rose higher than ever, speakeasies multiplied, people Charlestoned, sang the latest Gershwin songs, gave each other tips on the stock market—and managed to bury the last memories of the Great War that had brought not only actual death into so many people's lives, but a death to their illusions as well.

In 1927, however, Gershwin teamed up with the brilliant playwright George S. Kaufman to do a very different kind of musical. It was to be a satire, something along the lines of the Gilbert and Sullivan operettas, with a gentle spoofing of the manners of the times. But Gershwin's would be harsher, more biting and with a grimmer subject—war itself.

Not having to write for girlie routines and other stock musical-comedy situations, Gershwin, for the first time in his career, could use music in a more developed way to comment on character—a sneer of trumpets, for instance, to point up the falseness of the hypocritical hero, or sarcastic discords in a marching song to indicate the cowardice and foolishness of the army that figured in the plot. For the first time, too, Gershwin was required to compose an extended finale for each act, with various characters expressing their emotions at the same time. Those numbers had to be linked together musically, just as in an opera.

Ira Gershwin was also delighted at the prospect of writing a whole evening of witty, satirical verses. To counterbalance the sharpness of the show, however, the two brothers decided to work in at least one romantic song. George looked through his portfolio of unused or discarded material and came upon the poignant "The Man I Love," which had been eliminated from *Lady Be Good*. He had played it at parties, and people always seemed to like it. Indeed, an English friend, Lady Mountbatten, who was a cousin by marriage of the Royal Family, was so crazy about the song that when she was about to leave New York after a visit, George gave her a specially autographed copy of it as a going-away present. Accordingly, "The Man I Love" was taken out of the portfolio, dusted off and worked neatly into the new musical.

After three years of undeserved oblivion, it looked at last as if the song might be discovered.

Strike Up the Band, as the satirical operetta was called,

opened on September 5, 1927, in one of the usual tryout cities, Philadelphia. The critics were indeed reminded of Gilbert and Sullivan, but they found that the "morbid, bitter, stinging" book went deeper than anything written by those two more gentle satirists. Nevertheless, they were enthusiastic over the wit and intelligence of this refreshingly different musical.

But what of the audience? They came to *Strike Up the Band* to be entertained, and here was a lot of talk about war. They expected a story of romance and young love but found that the hero was a middle-aged president of a cheese factory. They came to laugh and forget their troubles but found that the laughs were all-too-strong reminders of what was wrong with man and the world that he had created. Night after night, the size of the audience diminished, and those people who bought tickets came away puzzled and dissatisfied. There was only one course open to the producers: *Strike Up the Band* was taken off the boards and never brought to New York at all. Back to Gershwin's portfolio went "The Man I Love," along with all the other songs from this, his first attempts to break away from a stereotyped Broadway show.

Ironically, two months later another "formula" musical written by Gershwin opened on Broadway to the usual raves. The show was called *Funny Face,* and soon everyone was singing the lovely title song and the charming

"'S Wonderful! 'S Marvelous—
You should care for me! . . ."

A month later a Jerome Kern musical came to New York. It was called *Show Boat* and had a powerful, often tragic story involving believable people, told through lovely and appropriate music. "A masterpiece," one critic said of it; others declared it to be America's first folk operetta.

If Jerome Kern had succeeded in writing a different kind of Broadway musical, why couldn't George Gershwin?

Restless, in need of new stimulus, George decided to go abroad early in 1928, first to London to see old friends, then on to Paris. With him went Ira, Ira's wife, Leonore, and George's kid sister, "Frankie." Gershwin had no definite plan in mind of what he might do. To be sure, the great French composer Maurice Ravel was in Paris. George had met him in New York and had played for him by the hour to the complete fascination of the Frenchman. Now George thought that Ravel might be willing to give him some instruction in composition. Walter Damrosch had also asked Gershwin to write some kind of symphonic work, and George had made a few preliminary sketches for it. Away from Broadway and in Europe, the continent with which he associated classical music, he might be inspired to complete the new work.

In England, the little party of Mr. and Mrs. I. Gershwin, Miss F. Gershwin and Mr. G. Gershwin went to a nightclub one evening and were startled to hear the band play "The Man I Love." How had this unknown Gershwin song managed to cross the ocean ahead of the Gershwins themselves? George did some sleuthing among his English friends and discovered the answer. Lady Mountbatten had taken the copy of the song that George had given her to a well-known London bandleader and had asked him to transcribe it for his orchestra. The song had caught on, and soon other bands and popular singers had taken it up.

The Gershwin party crossed to Paris on March 25, 1928,

and were amazed to discover that "The Man I Love" was being played and sung there too. What a curious twist, they thought, that a cousin of the British Royal Family should have turned out to be a successful song plugger!

For a number of years the exhilarating French capital had been a mecca for Americans attempting to absorb a culture older than their native one. The authors Ernest Hemingway and Gertrude Stein had come to live there, and F. Scott Fitzgerald was frequently about. Almost any really serious American composer—Aaron Copland, for instance—came to study at the Fontainebleau School of Music just outside of Paris. And then there were the Americans who came to Paris not so much for its culture as for the good food, favorable rate of exchange and general good times the city provided in that era of good times. Paris, at that period, was also a refuge for Russians who had found life under the new Communist regime intolerable, including composers such as Igor Stravinsky and Sergei Prokofiev.

No sooner had the Gershwins arrived than they were whirled into the musical and social life of the great city; if Gershwin was eager to extract new experience and inspiration from Paris, Paris was equally anxious to meet and honor him. Six days after his arrival, George discovered that the *Rhapsody in Blue* was to be performed by a leading orchestra with not one but two pianists dividing up the solo sections. The Gershwin party decided to attend. Unfortunately, the performance turned out to be terrible: the fast tempos were taken at a funeral pace, the rhythms were all off and Ira, who alternately giggled and squirmed with embarrassment, was certain that a banjo had played the same chord throughout the whole piece. George couldn't bear to listen and ducked out to the bar to console himself with a few drinks and to wait for the chorus of boos.

Imagine his astonishment when Ira came rushing in with the news that the whole house was cheering and calling for the composer to make an appearance. What the Gershwins had not realized was that however bad the performance of the *Rhapsody* had been, the work was new and different. "How they knew George was in the audience was a mystery to me as we had only heard about the concert that morning," Ira Gershwin jotted down in his diary. "An encore was announced," continued the entry ". . . of all things . . . a verse and three choruses of 'Do, Do, Do' from *Oh Kay*. This went with great éclat and the audience wanted more. It was the first time," wrote Ira, "that I ever heard of an encore by soloists at a symphony program."

Deems Taylor, the music critic and an admirer of Gershwin, happened to be in Paris at the time and heard of George's appearance at the concert. "If there's a bow to be taken," Taylor remarked tartly, "leave it to George to be there."

Because of the Gershwins' visit, there was a veritable festival of Gershwin music in Paris that spring. Soon after the performance of the *Rhapsody,* Frankie Gershwin was engaged by a fashionable nightclub to sing some of her older brother's songs. On the opening night George himself accompanied her. Not long after that, the famous ballet dancer Anton Dolin choreographed a new work, *The Rhapsody in Blue,* in which the two protagonists, Jazz and Classical Music, struggled to win out over one another. George, who was in the audience for the premiere, must have been pleased to see that after considerable difficulties Jazz finally won.

Then, at the end of May, the pianist and composer Dimitri

Tiomkin boldly engaged the huge Paris Opera House to present the French premiere of the Concerto in F with himself as soloist. He also scheduled a second program which included the *Rhapsody*. Tiomkin had been planning these concerts for some time and had come to Gershwin when they were both still in New York to borrow the only existing orchestrated version of the Concerto. During their meeting George managed to slip in a few minutes of playing for Tiomkin, but to Tiomkin's amazement Gershwin never asked him to play nor showed any interest as to whether he was competent enough to perform the difficult Concerto.

"He seemed to take it as a matter of course that the place at the keyboard was his," writes Tiomkin, in his amusing book of reminiscences, *Please Don't Hate Me*. "That was typical. He always put himself forward, amiable and smiling. With company at a restaurant, he'd walk in first with a gracious air, as a king might, taking the first place as his royal prerogative. At a party where eminent persons were present he'd go to the piano and play all evening, never thinking of making way for anyone else. He had a supreme self-confidence that may sound egotistical, but it was always accompanied by his courtesy and charm. He thought it acceptable to all, and it was."

Tiomkin also describes how the staid, rather conservative members of the Paris Opera orchestra were shocked at being asked to perform what they considered vulgar American jazz works. Since they prided themselves on performing difficult modern music by composers such as Stravinsky, they somewhat unwillingly managed to render the necessary jazz syncopations under the careful rehearsing of the conductor, Vladimir Golschmann. But when Golschmann produced a number of brown derby hats and told the trumpeters that they must place them over the bells of their instruments and wave them to produce the "wah-wah" effect demanded by the composer, it was too much. They indignantly refused to submit to such vulgarity. Tiomkin rushed to consult Gershwin. What were they to do? George was amused but pointed out that the score called for "dirty" trumpet playing and "dirty" trumpet playing there had to be.

Tiomkin thought and thought and finally came up with an idea. He took the hats to a jewelry shop and had them painted gold, "a gilt coating," he says, "that shone like the sun. Now they looked magnificent, fit for the archangel Gabriel and his trumpet."

The next day when the gleaming derbies were redistributed to the trumpeters, they blinked their eyes in amazement. Surely it would not be beneath their dignity to blow notes into objects of such dazzling splendor. Soon their trumpets were making a sound as pleasingly dirty as the composer could want.

The two concerts at the Opera created a tremendous stir in Paris, and capacity audiences received them with wild enthusiasm. "The orchestra may not have been as hot as a Harlem jazz session," Tiomkin recalls, "but it played the blue measures with enough of a swing and much more elegance." And, he adds, "It was something to see the stately musicians manipulating their golden derbies." Because of these concerts, Gershwin became famous all over Europe and was treated with the utmost respect—in a way that he was not in the United States—by the most famous European musicians, who regarded him as far and away America's most important composer.

Among these musicians was Maurice Ravel, with whom

Gershwin renewed his acquaintance and who was again enthralled by George's playing. There is a story—no one will absolutely swear that it is true—that when George asked Ravel if he could study with him the French composer refused, saying, "Why make a second-rate Ravel out of a first-rate Gershwin?" Curiously, though Gershwin stood in great awe of Ravel, Ravel, in the end, was more affected by Gershwin: certainly Ravel's two piano concertos, as well as his sonata for violin and piano, were all directly influenced by Gershwin's *Rhapsody in Blue* and Concerto in F.

There is another story—again not absolutely known to be true—that Gershwin then went to Stravinsky and asked to study with him. "How much money do you earn a year?" the great composer wanted to know. Gershwin named a figure between two and three hundred thousand dollars. "My dear man," Stravinsky replied, "let me take lessons from you."

Another composer whom Gershwin met at this time was Prokofiev, who though not impressed by the *Rhapsody in Blue*—"a series of thirty-two bar choruses rather badly strung together"—became more favorably disposed toward George's talents when he heard him play. George could go far, Prokofiev predicted, if he would leave "dollars and dinners" alone.

It was excellent advice, but difficult to follow—particularly when it came to the dinners. As the man of the hour, Gershwin was asked out everywhere. At a time when little enough excuse was needed for throwing a party, Paris turned his visit into one long blowout. For his part, he had all the normal American reactions to staying in the city—delight at its lovely boulevards, its buildings with their ironwork balconies, its pretty parks turning green in the spring; amazement at the aggressive way of the taxis with their impudent-sounding horns; and occasional nostalgia for America and American ways. He fell in love with a charming countess and just as quickly fell out again. All of these experiences George began to record musically in the symphonic work that he had been asked to write by Walter Damrosch, and on which he somehow found time to continue working. By June, the new piece was sufficiently advanced for him to let *The New York Times* announce that it would be played by the New York Symphony Society during the coming season. The composition was a kind of tone poem, "programmatic only in a general way," declared the composer, even though he had given it the title, *An American in Paris*.

Meanwhile, the American in Paris left for another famous and musical European city, Vienna. Here, too, he was feted and made much of. Orchestras in cafés would strike up themes from the *Rhapsody in Blue* when he entered. He met the leading Austrian composers of the day, ranging from Emmerich Kálmán, who wrote lighthearted operettas, to Alban Berg, who composed strange and difficult-to-comprehend atonal music. He also paid a call on the elderly widow of the waltz king, Johann Strauss, who plied him with delicious cups of chocolate and invited him for an enormous sum of money to buy the original score of her husband's most famous operetta, *Die Fledermaus*.

By the end of the summer, refreshed and stimulated, he was back in New York. There he found the popular new invention, the radio, had turned out to be a tremendously successful song-plugging device. And what song was it plugging? None other than "The Man I Love," which had come back across the Atlantic from Europe to become a great hit. In the first quarter of 1928 alone, it sold 60,000 copies in sheet music and 162,518 records. The song, of course, has become almost a classic. In form, with its accompaniment of a descending chromatic scale, it resembles a *lied* by the great German composer Hugo Wolf. Other musicologists have compared it to a sonata by Grieg. Whether Gershwin was familiar with those works is not known, nor does it matter. The song is purest Gershwin. As his brother Ira has said, "Friends tell me when they are abroad and request 'Play something by Gershwin' in some nightclub or café, invariably the first number played is 'The Man I Love.' "

Gershwin completed his orchestration of *An American in Paris* halfway through November, and the world premiere was scheduled for December 13, 1928. Anticipation ran high. Had Gershwin at last written a truly great piece of music? And would he—as in Europe—finally be treated by the critics as a serious composer, indeed, as America's greatest?

An American in Paris was presented with César Franck's Symphony in D Minor and the "Magic Fire" music from Richard Wagner's *Die Walküre*. The usual untypical Carnegie Hall audience turned out to hear it and, as was so often the case, took Gershwin's newest composition to their hearts at once. It would be difficult to understand how anyone could not respond to this most amiable and delightful of works. In it was all of George's Paris experience—delight at the Parisian boulevards, the taxi horns, the trees budding in the parks, the quick dalliance with the pretty countess, the nostalgia for home. It was G. Gershwin in Paris, but it was also *any* American in Paris. So it always will be as long as there are Americans to go to the great French city and orchestras equipped with a rattle, two tom-toms, four automobile horns, a wood block and a wire brush to play the work.

Yet incredible as it now seems, the critics were, if anything,

The Philharmonic-Symphony Society of New York

FOUNDED 1842

1928 - EIGHTY-SEVENTH SEASON - 1929

CARNEGIE HALL

Thursday Evening, December 13, 1928

AT EIGHT-THIRTY

Friday Afternoon, December 14, 1928

AT TWO-THIRTY

2338TH AND 2339TH CONCERTS

Under the Direction of

WALTER DAMROSCH

PROGRAM

1. FRANCK....................Symphony in D minor
   - I. Lento; allegro non troppo
   - II. Allegretto
   - III. Allegro non troppo

INTERMISSION

2. LEKEU....................Adagio for Strings

3. GERSHWIN....................“An American in Paris”
   (First performance anywhere)

4. WAGNER....................Magic Fire Scene, from “Die Walküre”

ARTHUR JUDSON, Manager
EDWARD ERVIN, Associate Manager

Owing to the great demand for Philharmonic-Symphony seats, which the management is unable to supply, it is requested that subscribers return tickets which cannot be used, to Philharmonic-Symphony Offices in Steinway Hall, or to the Box Office, Carnegie Hall, to be sold for the benefit of Orchestra Pension Fund

Those who wish to obtain the scores of any of the works on this program for home study should apply at the 58th Street Branch of the New York Public Library, 121 East 58th Street, which has a large collection of music available for circulation

more querulous and disputatious than before.

First Critic: "The best piece of modern music since Gershwin's Concerto in F."

Second Critic: "Nauseous claptrap . . . patchy, thin, vulgar, long-winded and inane."

Third Critic: "Engaging, ardent, unpredictable."

Fourth Critic: "Blunt banality—ballyhoo vulgarity."

Fifth Critic: "Material gain in workmanship and structure."

Sixth Critic: "Will anyone remember *An American in Paris* in twenty years' time?"

It is hard to understand how some of the critics could have so completely damned such a gay, amusing and altogether winning piece of music. Was it because they recognized Gershwin's extraordinary talent and were impatient that it produced nothing profound? Inspiration, technical proficiency, skillful use of the orchestra were all there; what was lacking was that deep note of human compassion, like a pedal point which sounds through all great works of music, whatever their moods.

By what means Gershwin could come to incorporate that note into his music was not clear. "I could wish for you an experience—not too prolonged—of that driving storm and stress of emotions, of that solitary wrestling with your own soul," his friend Otto Kahn had said. Yet no such experience seemed to befall him. Would he never write anything more than sometimes jaunty, sometimes sad, always charming pieces of music—but music that just fell short of greatness?

8 / Of Thee I Sing (Baby)

"IF HE SAW you juggling two coffee pots he would start practicing to be a juggler," one of Gershwin's best friends has recalled of the composer. "By evening he would be the best coffee-pot juggler in the world." Whatever Gershwin undertook, he always did with the utmost intensity and absorption. When he began to play golf, for example, he could only think, talk, dream about golf. Soon he was shooting in the low eighties, but the effect on his composing was slightly disastrous. "If I expect to write more music, I shall have to curb my love for golf," he wrote ruefully to a friend, adding, "unless some far-seeing golf club will place a Steinway at each tee."

In 1928 George decided to break away from total family living. He rented a penthouse on the seventeenth floor of a building on Riverside Drive with a sweeping view of the Hudson River. Ira and his wife installed themselves in the apartment next to it, and the brothers' terraces adjoined. George had his apartment decorated in the latest modern style with lots of chromium furniture. There was a well-equipped gymnasium in which he could work out and a strange, silver-colored upright piano.

Because he liked boxing, he bought original lithographs by George Bellows of scenes in the ring. Because he liked the lithographs, he became interested in how they were drawn.

And because he never did anything except wholeheartedly, under the guidance of his cousin, the painter Henry Botkin, he took up painting and drawing himself.

As Gershwin month after month worked at his easel with the same almost demoniac energy he brought to his composing and playing, it began to emerge that here was no dilettante artist relaxing in a world apart from keys and key signatures, but a serious, highly gifted painter. One of the most astonishing facts about George Gershwin is that when, after his death, an exhibition of his paintings was held in New York, a leading critic wrote: "He was not actually great as a painter, but that was merely because he had not yet had the time—but he was distinctly on the way to that goal. He had all the aptitudes. . . . If the soul be great, all the expressions emanating from the soul must be great."

Gershwin worked best as a portraitist, and the studies of his father, of Jerome Kern and of the novelist DuBose Heyward are telling characterizations of people he knew and loved well. Gershwin did two famous self-portraits. In one he wears a checked sweater against a background of rich, vivid colors; the other is a strange composition of himself wearing a top hat, white tie and tails, painting himself standing at an easel. Like an image repeated in a series of mirrors, it has all the mercilessness and coldness that mirrors have. Asked about his approach to painting, Gershwin once said, "I paint by ear. I compose my paintings as I compose music."

The more he painted, the more he learned about painting. This, in turn, caused him to buy works of art. His eye was discerning, his taste very much his own. As in his music, he was a man of his time, and he bought works mostly by twentieth-century artists. He liked strong pictures with bold colors. Rouault, with his sad clowns depicted in stained-glass

George Gershwin painted a self-portrait in top hat, white tie, and tails.
ARTHUR GERSHWIN COLLECTION, PHOTOGRAPH BY PETER A. JULEY & SON

hues, was Gershwin's favorite artist, but perhaps the most famous picture that Gershwin ever bought was Picasso's poignant study of a young man at a café table, "The Absinthe Drinker," for which he paid fifteen hundred dollars. After his death the picture was bought for the Museum of Modern Art in New York City for fifteen thousand dollars, and it can be seen there still.

With the coming of 1929 America entered what turned out to be the last year of the dizzy, high-riding jazz era. Already warnings had been sounded. The stock market was dangerously inflated. People could boast of owning huge fortunes, but they were mostly on paper. Suppose that everyone, from reasons of caution, decided to turn their paper stocks into hard cash all at the same time? Where would there be anyone willing to buy, except at vastly reduced prices? The warnings were cried but no one paid any heed. America was like George Gershwin, brilliantly endowed, filled with self-confidence, completely optimistic. Like Gershwin, the country had had one or two flops and out-of-town closings in its history—but never a really drastic setback to make it doubt its powers.

Seventeen stories up in the building on Riverside Drive the parties were brighter, livelier, later than ever. Often they would begin in Ira's apartment and at some point in the evening spread over to George's. Among the regulars of the Gershwins' circle was their old friend the writer S. N. Behrman, the violinist Mischa Levitzki, the gifted musician Kay Swift and George Gershwin's critic champion, Samuel Chotzinoff. The atmosphere was warm, the music gay and the talk—sharp.

It was at one of these parties that another Gershwin regular, possibly the most sharp-tongued of them all, Oscar Levant, got his much-quoted revenge against Gershwin for an incident that had once happened while they were traveling together. The two men were in a sleeping car bound for Pittsburgh. They had been talking about music and Levant was looking forward to staying up half the night discussing his favorite subject, when Gershwin suddenly eased himself into the lower berth, saying to the pianist, "Lower berth, upper berth. That's the difference between genius and talent. Good night, Oscar."

One evening when George was playing at one of his own parties, reveling as usual in the feeling of being the center of attention, Oscar Levant went over to him and said in his ear, "Tell me, George, if you had to do it all over, would you fall in love with yourself again?"

Gershwin throve on worship—indeed required it. "In order to create pure and poetic music and greater works of art," a friend once said about him, "George needed praise and admiration as a flower needs sunshine and rain." In some curious way Gershwin worshipped himself—a George Gershwin who, as in his self-portrait, stood outside himself and admired the extraordinary and mysterious talent of George Gershwin. He often spoke of himself in the third person. "Gershwin's music is terrific," he was heard to say. Who could deny it?

However, 1929 proved to be one of the least rewarding of the Gershwin years. Early in July he returned to Broadway with songs for *Show Girl,* produced by Florenz Ziegfeld of "Follies" fame. The musical had attractive stars, an *American in Paris* blues ballet and one of Gershwin's most charming songs, "Liza," but none of these assets was enough to prevent it from being the great Ziegfeld's greatest failure.

Sandwiched between rehearsals of *Show Girl* were renewed visits to the studio of Edward Kilenyi. George was off on another tack—conducting. He had arranged to conduct *An American in Paris* and to appear as soloist in the *Rhapsody in Blue* at one of the outdoor concerts held every summer at New York's Lewisohn Stadium. Kilenyi taught him the essentials of using a baton and sent him home to practice his technique using phonograph records. On the night of July 8, one of the largest audiences in the history of the Stadium concerts turned out to hear him make a highly successful debut as a conductor. Considering how many Broadway shows Gershwin had been connected with, it seems odd that he had never thought of conducting before. Thereafter, he frequently took his place on the podium using a technique, his friend and biographer Isaac Goldberg tells us, that was unmistakably his own. "George conducts with a baton, with his cigar, with his shoulders, with his eyes . . . a gentle polyrhythm of his entire body. He sings with the principals and chorus; he whistles; he imitates the various instruments of the orchestra; nothing but a sense of propriety, indeed, keeps him from leaping over the footlights and getting right into the show."

The failure of *Show Girl* proved to be a dire prophecy of what was to happen to America. Some days after the musical closed the stock market collapsed. In a few hours, people, who on paper seemed to have wealth had, in fact, nothing at all. Among those who suffered terrible losses was Florenz Ziegfeld. In his desperation he blamed Gershwin for the failure of *Show Girl* and refused to pay him royalties for his songs. Gershwin was normally the most generous of men. He never retained a lawyer on a yearly basis the way most people with his income do, and he had never been involved in any legal controversies. Now, reluctantly, he was forced to sue Ziegfeld.

During the fall of 1929, while Gershwin was at work on a

revised version of the satire *Strike Up the Band,* there was much talk that the stock market break had been only temporary, and a few rallies encouraged false hopes. But as the new year came on, a feeling gradually spread through the country that prosperity was not going to come back. The good-time years were over; bank failures, closed factories and bread lines announced the spirit of the new decade.

It is in the bitter laughter of satire that a grim people find release. *Strike Up the Band,* Gershwin's first satirical operetta, opened on Broadway in January, 1930, and suddenly there was an audience to appreciate this different kind of musical, with its plot involving tariffs, international treaties and big business. "Of all things in the world," exclaimed a newspaper columnist over *Strike Up the Band,* "here is a bitter, rather good satirical attack on war, genuine propaganda at times, sung and danced on Broadway to standing room only."

Strike Up the Band was an important development for both the Broadway musical and Gershwin as a composer. Gone were the trite plot situations, the routine spots for dances and specialty numbers, the evening of totally brainless entertainment. The audience was expected to (and did) bring their own wits to bear on what was taking place on the stage. Their standard of taste had been given a much-needed boost. Soon they would no longer put up with the other, formula kind of musical comedy. They would want, instead, an integrated, intelligent evening of musical theatergoing such as *Show Boat,* and now *Strike Up the Band* proved that Broadway could provide.

As for Gershwin, *Strike Up the Band* was his first chance at a "complete" musical, the first time he could make really telling musical characterizations and comments, the first

George Gershwin made his debut as a conductor at Lewisohn Stadium on July 8, 1929, and appeared again as guest conductor and soloist on August 26. CULVER PICTURES, INC.

opportunity he had had to write extended musical numbers, ensembles and finales—just the way an operatic composer would. He did well by these opportunities. In the years to come he would do even better.

As the Depression deepened, the wry, the sarcastic, the sometimes-bitter moods that spread over Broadway and its songs brought out the best in Ira Gershwin. For many years people had recognized that a Gershwin song owed part of its unique quality to the fact that it was by Ira as well as George Gershwin. The partnership of the two brothers was something very special. Completely different in temperament, they seemed to understand one another almost without having to speak. In his *Lyrics on Several Occasions,* Ira has given us some fascinating glimpses of how he and his brother wrote their famous songs.

They were in Hollywood working on the movie musical *A Damsel in Distress.* "We had finished three or four songs," Ira recalls. "One night I was in the living room, reading. About 1 A.M. George returned from a party . . . took off his dinner jacket, sat down at the piano . . . 'How about some work? Got any ideas?' 'Well, there's one spot we might do something about a fog . . . how about *a foggy day in London* or maybe *foggy day in London town?*' 'Sounds good. . . . I like it better with *town'* and he was off immediately on the melody. We finished the refrain, words and music in less than an hour. ('Do, Do, Do' is the only other . . . in so short a time.) Next day the song still sounded good so we started on a verse. . . .

"All I had to say was 'George, how about an Irish verse?' and he sensed instantly the degree of wistful loneliness I meant. Generally, whatever mood I thought was required, he, through his instinct and inventiveness, could bring my hazy musical vision into focus. . . . When George had many tunes on tap for me and I couldn't recall exactly the start of a particular one I wanted to discuss, I would visualize the vocal line and my forefinger would draw an approximation of its curves in the air. And more often than not he would know the tune I meant. . . .

"Needless to say this sort of affinity between composer and lyricist comes only after long association between the two"[1] —a rare understatement.

Ira Gershwin's simple, unsentimental and highly sophisticated way with words contributed much to the atmosphere of a Gershwin song. He always strove for naturalness, the casual, partly slangy way in which people ordinarily converse. One of his favorite devices is to use clichés—"flash in the pan," "things have come to a pretty pass," "lay one's cards on the table"—in his lyrics, which, as he himself points out, far from sounding trite and worn out, are somehow revitalized when set to music. Called upon to write a lyric to suit a soupy situation in which, for example, a pair of lovers are forced to separate, Ira comes up with most unsoupy lines that point up the situation much more believably and touchingly by their understatement:

> The way you wear your hat,
> The way you sip your tea,
> The mem'ry of all that——
> No, no! They can't take that away from me! [2]

Writing words for a "straight" love song always made him uncomfortable, and he regarded his lines for "Love Walked

[1] Reprinted by permission of Mr. Ira Gershwin.

[2] Copyright © 1937 by Gershwin Publishing Corporation. Copyright renewed. Used by permission of the publisher.

In," one of George's loveliest melodies, as "pompous in an unobvious way, but . . . still pompous."

A satirical operetta such as *Strike Up the Band* offered Ira the opportunity to write in just the light, wry vein that he liked. One of its most amusing numbers was called "I'm a Typical Self-made American" and gave Ira a chance to take more than one shot at just that, a typical, smug, self-made American.

> "I got a job and worked both day and night at it,
> And all the day I never watched the clock.
> The big boss thought I was so very bright at it
> That when he died he left me all the stock.
> I was there when opportunity came to knock!"

boasted the hero, while the chorus reverently repeated,

> "He is a typical, typical, typical, self-made American!"

The next Gershwin musical, *Girl Crazy,* reverted to the old kind of twenties formula musical with a plot about a millionaire playboy who is sent west by his family to a dude ranch to keep him out of trouble. But George's tunes and Ira's sparkling lines were among their best. Ginger Rogers had just made a name for herself in the movies and starred in the show, while jazz fans recall *Girl Crazy* with awe because playing in the orchestra were Benny Goodman, Gene Krupa, Glenn Miller, Jack Teagarden and Red Nichols. But it was a virtually unknown singer in a secondary part who triumphed over all these famous names on the opening night.

At about five minutes to ten, when a vigorous, lusty brunette came out in a low-cut red blouse and black satin skirt and, leaning against the proscenium arch, let loose with a "kootchy" number called "Sam and Delilah," the audience screamed and yelled and made so much noise that young Ethel Merman thought "something had fallen out of the loft onto the stage." She had been an unknown until she went to audition for Gershwin who was so impressed by her singing that he asked her if she wanted him to make any changes in the songs that he had written for his new show. Miss Merman, flabbergasted at such a question from the great George Gershwin, could only think to tell him that they would "do very nicely."

The score of *Girl Crazy* contained a number of all-time hits, including the exhilarating "I Got Rhythm," the appealing "But Not for Me," and the burlesque hayseed song "Bidin' My Time," in which Ira derived great satisfaction in rhyming "time" with "I'm." Still another hit was "Embraceable You," which became a great favorite of Mr. Gershwin. He would ask George to play it when company was present, then thump his chest and beam around the room at the line "Come to papa—come to papa—do!"

Girl Crazy ran for thirty-four weeks on Broadway, a record at that time, for like everything else in America, the theater had been hard hit by the Depression. It was expensive to produce a Broadway show, and there was less and less money to be gotten from backers, just as few people could afford the high prices for tickets. The movies, on the other hand, which reached millions and millions of people, could charge as little as a dime for a double feature and still make incredible profits, while providing America with forgetfulness and cheer in the never-never world of the silver screen.

Since the movies now had a voice, it was inevitable that they would want some Gershwin songs to sing, and so, toward the end of 1930, the brothers Gershwin set off for

Hollywood. They lived seven weeks in a house that the great star Greta Garbo had previously occupied and wrote four songs for a now-forgotten movie (George also wrote a dream sequence for voice and orchestra and an orchestral sequence describing the sounds of a city), for which they received a hundred thousand dollars. "Hollywood is okay . . ." George wrote back to a friend, "that is as far as the Gershwins are concerned . . . My face is tanned—I still have indigestion—there are many beautiful women out here—I shot an eighty-six at the Rancho Golf Club the other day . . ." And as an afterthought, "Our picture is practically written."

Composing music for the movies—turning it out, so to speak, by the yard—was unworthy of Gershwin and he knew it. He tried to make something out of the Hollywood experience by taking some of the themes of the city orchestral sequence in the picture and weaving them into an orchestral work which he called *Second Rhapsody*. "Nearly everybody comes back from California with a western tan and a pocketful of moving-picture money," he told an interviewer. "I decided to come back with both those things and a serious composition."

Unfortunately, the Hollywood approach to composing seemed to have infected Gershwin's musical imagination. A year later, when the *Second Rhapsody* was given its premiere by Serge Koussevitzky and the Boston Symphony Orchestra, the critics, while praising Gershwin's increased musical craftsmanship, found that the work lacked the drive and inspiration of his earlier pieces. Time has upheld their opinion. Today, the *Second Rhapsody* is Gershwin's least played, least popular serious work.

Back in busy, fast-paced New York, which he loved better than any place on earth, Gershwin set to work on a second musical satire by the authors of *Strike Up the Band*—with Ira, of course, in charge of the lyrics. This time the subject was a presidential campaign and intrigues in Washington following the election. Into the madcap plot the authors managed to work a bathing beauty contest, a romance centering around a girl who can bake corn muffins and a debate in the Senate as to whether a long-overdue pension should be voted for Paul Revere's horse, Jenny. There was also a wrestling match, a torchlight parade and an endearing portrait of that forgotten man the Vice-President, who is only able to get into the White House by joining a guided tour.

Among all the goings-on the authors were able to get off some very sharp observations on campaign practices and promises, the corruption of political bosses, the foolish debates that can take place in Congress and the confusion of the Supreme Court rulings. Gershwin was right in there with them, using music to mock and burlesque, point up and put over what was taking place on the stage. Whether it was writing a rousing campaign chant, "Wintergreen for President," or using a pseudo-operatic style to indicate the pomposity of the senators or setting Ira's ingenious lines that President Wintergreen sings,

> Some girls can bake a pie,
> Made up of prunes and quinces,
> Some make an oyster fry——
> Others are good at blintzes.
> Some lovely girls have done
> Wonders with turkey stuffin's,
> But I have found the one
> Who can really make corn muffins!

Gershwin got the perfect musical touch every time. The

result, *Of Thee I Sing,* was the most brilliant and successful musical he ever wrote.

The show tried out in Boston and opened in New York on the day after Christmas, 1931. The critics in both cities went wild.

FIRST CRITIC: "One of the drollest satirical operettas of all time."

SECOND CRITIC: "It has very nearly succeeded in liberating the musical comedy stage from the mawkish and feeble-minded formula that has long been considered inevitable."

THIRD CRITIC: "It has set a fresh pattern for the American musical stage."

SECOND CRITIC: "It is funnier than the government and not nearly so dangerous."

In many ways the shrewdest judge of Gershwin was Gershwin himself. "Ira and I have never been connected with a show of which we were prouder," George told a friend about *Of Thee I Sing.*

The show had opened at a moment when America, desperately in need of a strong government, was faltering under a weak one. People crowded in to see this clever musical that humorously pointed up the follies and wrongs of their political system and governing bodies. *Of Thee I Sing* ran for 441 performances, and a second company toured the country simultaneously for eight months of the run. In the spring of 1932, *Of Thee I Sing* received the unprecedented tribute of being awarded the Pulitzer Prize as the best play of the year. No musical had ever been so honored. "This award may seem unusual," read the citation, "but the play is unusual . . . Its effect on the stage promises to be very considerable, because musical plays are always popular, and by injecting satire and point into them, a very large public is reached."

Of Thee I Sing was revived in 1952 to the usual critical cheers. The satire had not lost its sting and the music sounded better than ever. There is every reason to suppose it will continue to reappear for as long as anyone likes musicals.

Of Thee I Sing was Gershwin's greatest Broadway success and his last. In the two years that followed its premiere, the plight of America grew steadily worse and unemployment mounted. In some extraordinary way Gershwin, the composer, seemed to mirror the decline. Perhaps it was also due to the fact that for the first time he experienced the feelings of loss and helplessness caused by the death of someone he loved. In May, 1932, ten days after *Of Thee I Sing* had been awarded the Pulitzer Prize, gentle, humorous Mr. Gershwin died of leukemia. The family wall that had always ringed George about and protected him had been broached; he with his nerve and vitality and self-assurance had been helpless to do anything about it.

Earlier that year Gershwin had visited Cuba and had been fascinated by the rhythms of the native dances and the strange percussion instruments, such as bongos, gourds and maracas, which were relatively unknown in America at that time. That summer he composed a lively *Cuban Overture,* which received its first performance on August 16, 1932, at Lewisohn Stadium. To make sure that the Cuban percussion instruments were used effectively, Gershwin drew sketches of them at places in the score where he wanted them to be played.

The *Cuban Overture* turned out to be minor Gershwin, full of the usual Gershwin charm, and was a curious forerunner of so much of the Latin American music that is popular today. Gershwin was particularly proud that the premiere took place in an all-Gershwin concert which broke every attendance record at the mammoth Stadium. All-Gershwin concerts have been a tradition there ever since and have continued to break attendance records.

Gershwin's only other musical output during 1932 was a book of piano transcriptions of his songs. As he explained in an introduction, "Playing my songs as frequently as I do at private parties, I have naturally been led to compose numerous variations upon them and to indulge the desire for complication and variety that every composer feels when he manipulates the same material over and over again." The book makes a fascinating and valuable record of how Gershwin played his own songs. It is not, in his words, "for little girls with little hands," since it makes the utmost demands in piano technique.

The following year saw two Gershwin failures on Broadway, *Pardon My English,* a return to the old kind of musical comedy, and *Let 'Em Eat Cake,* a third satirical operetta. But with the latter, the author tried to hit at too much, or perhaps with mounting trouble all over the world, there was too much to hit at. Fascism, communism, the overthrow of the United States Government, big business, the League of Nations were all somehow worked into the plot. "Their hatreds have triumphed over their sense of humor," Brooks Atkinson said of the authors in *The New York Times.* Gershwin did his best, but it is an axiom in the musical theater that not even the most gifted composer, neither a Mozart nor a Gershwin, can win over a bad story. Both musicals contained some good Gershwin songs—but by then it was clear that Gershwin could write a good song practically in his sleep. What was not so clear was whether he could and would write anything more of major importance.

There is no doubt that Gershwin knew what heights he

was capable of reaching, yet some other part of his nature bedeviled him into accepting easy, well-paid musical assignments that offered him no challenge. When an artist realizes his true capacity and knows that he is not fulfilling it, depression inevitably sets in. By 1934, the old cocky, I-can-lick-the-world Gershwin spirit was wavering like a candle in a draft. Outwardly, he appeared to be the same famous and brilliant composer with all the success and fame and admiration that he could possibly want. That year, for the first time, he had his own radio program, "Music by Gershwin." He also went on a transcontinental tour as piano soloist with an orchestra conducted by Charles Previn. For these concerts he wrote the entertaining variations on "I Got Rhythm" which are still played on programs of light music today. All over the country audiences crowded into concert halls to see and hear the great Gershwin.

Until then, he had fed on success. It had been enough to keep him going. Now, suddenly, it was no longer nourishing. Friends had often predicted that when he grew older he would suffer from his inability to have anything more than a casual love affair. At thirty-five, he now had to face the fact that he was alone—always in company with Ira, to be sure, but Ira was married. So were his other brother and his sister Frankie. His stomach continued to bother him. He grew depressed. "I can't eat. I can't sleep. I can't fall in love," he complained to friends. In an effort to help his plight, he went to a psychiatrist—but there was, in fact, no treatment for a musical genius who was not fulfilling that genius.

"I could wish for you an experience—not too prolonged—of that driving storm and stress of the emotions, of that solitary wrestling with your own soul . . ."

Now he knew death and a sense of aloneness. All around

him in his own country there was deprivation and despair. And from Europe came sickening reports of prejudice and atrocities against people of his own race. Life could not be for him the bright thing, as gay and glittering as a sign atop a Broadway theater, that it had once seemed. In the darkness beyond the light he knew now there was suffering.

And in that knowledge George Gershwin at last created a great work of music.

9 / Porgy and Bess

"PORGY LIVED IN the Golden Age. Not the Golden Age of a remote and legendary past . . . but an age when men, not yet old, were boys in an ancient, beautiful city that time had forgotten before it destroyed."

One night in 1926, restless and unable to sleep, George Gershwin picked up a best-selling novel that someone had brought into the house on 103rd Street. Unlike Ira, George never cared much for reading. But from the opening lines of this book, which was called *Porgy,* straight to the end, Gershwin found himself gripped by the elemental, tragic story laid in Charleston, South Carolina, which had been told in a very spare, elemental way. The characters were almost entirely Negroes, and the author, DuBose Heyward, had not treated them as stock comic figures or piteous figures of injustice, but as fully rounded, believable human beings. Heyward was a white man, but a native of Charleston—and was an artist. He had understood his characters well—the lonely Porgy, "by nature a dreamer," with his strong hands and crippled body, and Bess, weak and reckless, but "with an air of pride" always showing in her bearing. Then there was Crown, "a stevedore with the body of a gladiator and a bad name," and the indolent, gaudily dressed dope peddler, Sportin' Life.

On and on into the night read Gershwin, and as he came to one vivid scene after another—the gambling game in which

Crown stabs Robbins, the rollicking picnic on Kittiwah Island, the terrifying hurricane—an idea began slowly to take shape in his mind. Gershwin's first attempt at a serious musical work had been *Blue Monday*, an opera with all-Negro characters, which jazz and blues idioms were particularly suited to portray. *Blue Monday* had failed, and one of the chief reasons was its weak story—

Porgy is not a long novel, but George was a slow reader and by the time he had finished, dawn was breaking over New York City. Rushing to his desk, George seized a piece of paper and wrote to DuBose Heyward, telling him how much he admired *Porgy* and asking if he would be interested in collaborating on a folk opera based on the novel at some future date. Technically, Gershwin explained, he did not feel he was ready to write a full-length opera yet, but he did want to find out Heyward's attitude toward such a plan and to speak for the rights to the book before anyone else did.

Heyward responded enthusiastically to Gershwin's letter, and the two men met. "My first impression of my collaborator remains with me and is singularly vivid," recalled the novelist a number of years later, ". . . A young man of enormous physical and emotional vitality, who possessed the faculty of seeing himself quite impersonally and realistically, and who knew exactly what he wanted and where he was going." Heyward was amazed that a composer who had already enjoyed such dazzling success "could appraise his talent with such complete detachment" and recognize that he was not quite ready to write a full-length opera. Nothing definite came from the meeting except that the two men liked each other and felt that one day when they were both prepared they could do an operatic version of *Porgy*.

Several years passed. The idea came up again, was enthusiastically discussed—and was dropped. Then in 1930 George Gershwin received a commission from the Metropolitan Opera Company to write an opera using any libretto that appealed to him. For the past twenty years the Met had been producing opera after opera by American composers, every one a poor imitation of the great French, Italian and German operas which made up the Met's repertory. None had had more than a mild success. Gershwin, with his usual musical astuteness, saw what the trouble was. "Where is the sense and where is the personal satisfaction in doing over again what has been done before, and done better?" he said to an interviewer. "When I think of a grand opera of my own, I simply cannot think in terms of Wagner or Verdi. Once and for all, Wagner wrote the overpowering music dramas. Once and for all, Verdi, the supreme melodist, wrote the breast-heaving, arm-brandishing orgies that will live on despite the high-browed critics. Why do, in pale imitativeness, what they did so superbly—and did because they were supremely themselves? I want, in turn, to be myself," he added in typical Gershwin style.

Yet if Gershwin chose *Porgy* as the subject of his opera, how could the Metropolitan produce it, since it would require an entirely Negro cast? At that time there wasn't a single Negro on the Met's roster. Gershwin looked around for other ideas for an opera, but could find nothing that suited him as well as *Porgy*. He was particularly annoyed when people suggested that a truly American opera should have a truly American subject—Indians. "The Indians," he spluttered, "are as obsolete as their wooden brothers that used to stand in front of the cigar stores."

So Gershwin continued to drift. Would writing an opera turn out to be just another unfulfilled dream? Three years later, Gershwin had a jolting communication from Heyward. Jerome Kern and Oscar Hammerstein II, the composers of *Show Boat*, were after him for the musical rights to *Porgy*. Their idea was to turn the book into a musical comedy using a cast in blackface, not to make it the all-Negro folk opera that Gershwin had suggested. Heyward would much rather work with Gershwin, but on the other hand, he had been hard hit by the Depression, and if George was never going to do anything about *Porgy* he could not afford to turn the other offer down. "I want you to tell me," he said bluntly to Gershwin, "if you are really going to write that opera—and *soon.*"

It was just the kind of pressuring that George needed to get him into action. In October, 1933, came a long-awaited announcement: George Gershwin was going to compose a folk opera based on DuBose Heyward's *Porgy*, which would be produced on Broadway with an all-Negro cast. "It's going to be a labor of love," he wrote to a friend after the contracts had been signed, "and I expect quite a few labor pains with it."

It is doubtful that he could have imagined then how much labor, how much love and how many pains the writing of the opera would cost him in the next two years.

For Gershwin, it was his greatest challenge. He brought to it the happy combination of his own musical genius, overwhelming vitality and enthusiasm and years of experience in the theater. "I want to be myself," he had declared, when it came to writing an opera—and "myself" he would be. At the same time the work must be in proper operatic form without any bow to Broadway conceptions. DuBose Heyward, for example, wanted to use spoken dialogue, but Gershwin refused. In opera, dialogue is set to music which makes the words of the characters more meaningful. However, he made one masterly compromise. The opera was about Negro life, therefore all the Negro characters would sing their speeches. But the few minor whites in the story would express themselves in a way alien to opera—by the spoken word.

DuBose Heyward lived in South Carolina and found it inconvenient to bring his wife and child to New York City. Gershwin was under contract to broadcast a radio program from New York every Sunday throughout the winter. With a thousand miles between them, the two men set to work to shape the necessary libretto for their opera.

By February, 1934, a certain amount of progress had been made. "I know you will be eager to see more of the script," Heyward wrote to Gershwin, "so I am sending the next two scenes herewith. . . . I think maybe the composition on the lyrics better wait until we get together. I have in mind something for them but I cannot well suggest it by writing, especially the boat song."

"I received your Second Act's script," Gershwin replied, "and think it is fine. I really think you are doing a magnificent job with the new libretto and I hope I can match it musically. I have been composing music for the First Act and I am starting with the songs and spirituals first."

The winter dragged on and the separation imposed a strain on both men. Heyward wrote to Gershwin, "I have been hearing you on the radio and the reception was so good it seemed as though you were in the room. In fact the illusion was so perfect I could hardly keep from shouting at you, 'Swell show, George, but what the hell is the news about PORGY! ! !' "

Soon it became clear that the composer and the librettist were being seriously hampered by working apart. "I am sort of at a deadlock," Heyward complained to Gershwin. "The storm scene must stand as it is with very few cuts in the dialogue. Musically it must be done when we are together. It must carry itself on the big scene when Crown sings against a spiritual and I can't do the lyrics until I get your ideas as to time."

"I was happy to get your letter with the 3rd Scene of Act II enclosed," Gershwin wrote back. "I think it is a very interesting and touching scene, although a bit on the long side. . . . You must make sure that the opera is not too long, as I am a great believer in not giving people too much of a good thing and I am sure you agree with this." He too, had been held up in his work by the enforced separation. "I would like to write the song that opens the 2nd Act, sung by Jake with the fish nets, but I don't know the rhythm you had in mind—especially for the answers of the chorus, so I would appreciate it if you would put dots and dashes over the lyrics and send it to me."

Gershwin's radio program was not finished until June. There was nothing to do but let the spring pass slowly by and try to carry on as best they could. Into the collaboration in his usual quiet, modest way slipped Ira, with his vast knowledge of the musical theater. Though DuBose Heyward was a poet, he had never written lyrics to be sung. As Ira himself has written, "It takes years and years of experience to know that such a note cannot take such a syllable, that many a poetic line can be unsingable, that many an ordinary line fitted into the proper musical phrase can sound like a million." Ira, then, became a polisher of the lyrics that Heyward wrote and general supervisor of the project as a whole. Because Ira was particularly good at writing snappy, sophisticated lyrics, he also was asked to write the words for Sportin' Life's wicked songs.

At last June came and George, in a high state of excitement, made plans for an extended stay in South Carolina near where Heyward lived. Once before, he had gone away from New York City and in comparative solitude and aloofness written his most deeply felt piece of symphonic music, the Concerto in F. This time, as a maturer artist and human being, he went to a place of even greater isolation at Folly Beach, on an island twelve miles from Charleston.

The previous year, George had moved into a new and even grander penthouse apartment on East 72nd Street. It contained a high-ceilinged living room, a paneled library, a gymnasium, an art studio and a special glass bar—all furnished in the best taste by one of New York's leading interior decorators. From these quarters, appropriate to America's first composer and New York's leading man-about-town, George moved into a primitive shack with an old iron bedstead and a few crumbling pieces of furniture. Drinking water had to be brought in five-gallon jugs from the mainland. An old upright piano, reminiscent of the first instrument that the Gershwin family had ever owned, was moved in, on which he could do his composing. Here, unshaven and clad mostly in a bathing suit, the Gershwin of the beautifully cut English suits and immaculate appearance lived by the sea and sand and under the hot sun and worked with an excitement bordering on ecstasy which he had never known before.

Outside the cabin, bull alligators roared in the swamps; there were great turtles lazing in the water; crickets raised their rasping din. Not only were the simple elements of

George Gershwin at the piano in his East 72nd Street penthouse. On the wall behind him is a portrait he painted of his grandfather.

CULVER PICTURES, INC.

nature there, to alternately stimulate and relax him, there were the Negroes themselves. On an adjacent island was a large population of primitive Gullah Negroes, "an inexhaustible source of folk material," as DuBose Heyward later recalled. He was amazed at how much the music of the Negro seemed to be inside Gershwin without George's ever having lived in the South. "As we sat listening to their spirituals, or watched a group shuffling before a cabin or country store, . . . to George it was more like a homecoming than an exploration. The quality in him which had produced the *Rhapsody in Blue* in the most sophisticated city in America, found its counterpart in the impulse behind the music and bodily rhythms of the simple Negro peasant of the South."

Heyward goes on to relate an incredible story about Gershwin. "The Gullah Negro prides himself on what he calls 'shouting.' This is a complicated rhythmic pattern beat out by feet and hands as an accompaniment to the spirituals and is indubitably an African survival. I shall never forget the night when, at a Negro meeting on a remote sea-island, George started 'shouting' with them. And eventually to their huge delight stole the show from their champion 'shouter.' I think that he is probably the only white man in America who could have done it."

Another night, the two men were about to enter a cabin that had been taken over by a group of Negroes for a prayer meeting. Gershwin, caught by the sound of the praying coming from inside, stayed Heyward's arm. It was a familiar enough sound to Heyward, but noticing the composer's excitement, he now listened anew. "It consisted," he writes, "of perhaps a dozen voices raised in loud rhythmic prayer. The odd thing about it was that while each had started at a different time, upon a different theme, they formed a clearly defined rhythmic pattern, and that this, with the actual words lost, and the inevitable pounding of the rhythm, produced an effect almost terrifying in its primitive intensity." This experience gave Gershwin the inspiration for the music of the second-act hurricane scene of his opera, in which he uses a number of prayers sung simultaneously to evoke the terror and faith of the inhabitants of Catfish Row in the midst of a mighty storm.

It is significant that DuBose Heyward described Gershwin's visit to Folly Island as "more like a homecoming than an exploration." Had he indeed come home to the simple, almost elemental life that he had known as a poor boy—a few necessary clothes, a nail on which to hang them, an old upright in the corner of the room on which to discover music and especially the music within himself? Here there was no flattering attention, nothing to feed his vanity, nobody to remind him of what a long way he had come up in the world. He had no reason to believe his new work would make much money: the public was well known to be suspicious of opera. But Gershwin had put worldliness away. For him, writing the opera was truly a labor of love. He had put himself completely and honestly into it and he was sure it was good. And that was enough.

In September, he returned to New York with the music for the opera more or less sketched out. He could write a delightful song in half an hour and earn a fortune by it. But to complete the complex choral passages, contrapuntal writing and orchestration of the opera took another whole year. Not until September 2, 1935, was he satisfied to date the manuscript and mark it "finished." When published, the vocal score was 559 pages long.

Through it all he had worked like a man in a trance. When it was done, happiness and pride in what he had accomplished bubbled out of him. Walking on the street with the score under his arm he met a friend. "Look what I've done!" he shouted waving around the bulky manuscript. When he was playing the fugue that accompanies the crap game in Act One to friends, his face suddenly lit up, his cigar tilted high with pride. "Get this. Gershwin writing fugues. What will the boys say next?"

A play had been made from DuBose Heyward's novel before the opera and Rouben Mamoulian had directed it. It was decided to bring him east from Hollywood, where he was now a well-known movie director, to stage this new incarnation of *Porgy*. Naturally, Mamoulian had never heard a note of the music, and George, with Ira assisting, decided to invite him to his apartment and give him an idea of what the score was like. This is how Mamoulian recalled one of the most deeply moving experiences of his life:

> It was rather amusing how all three of us were trying to be nonchalant and poised that evening, yet were trembling with excitement. The brothers handed me a tall highball and put me in a comfortable leather arm chair. George sat down at the piano while Ira stood over him like a guardian angel. George's hands went up in the air about to strike the shining keys. Halfway down he changed his mind, turned to me and said, "Of course, Rouben, you must understand it's very difficult to play this score. As a matter of fact it's really impossible. Can you play Wagner? Well, this is like Wagner." [It is interesting to recall that Richard Wagner used to play and sing his latest music dramas through to friends when he had completed them, just as Gershwin was about to do with Rouben Mamoulian.]

I assured George that I understood. Up went his nervous hands again and the next second I was listening to the opening "piano music" in the opera. I found it so exciting, so full of color and so provocative in its rhythms that after this first "piano section" was over, I jumped out of my arm chair and interrupted George to tell him how much I liked it. Both brothers were as happy as children to hear words of praise, though heaven knows, they should have been used to them by then.

When my explosion was over and they went back to the piano, they both blissfully closed their eyes before they continued with the lovely "Summertime" song. George played with the most beatific smile on his face. He seemed to float on the waves of his own music with the Southern sun shining on him. Ira sang—he threw back his head with abandon, his eyes closed, and sang like a nightingale. In the middle of the song George couldn't bear it any longer and took over the singing from him. To describe George's face as he sang "Summertime" is something beyond my capacity as a writer . . .

So it went on. George was the orchestra and played the parts. Ira sang the other half. Ira was also frequently the "audience." It was touching to see how he, while singing, would become so overwhelmed with admiration for his brother, that he would look from him to me with half-open eyes and pantomime with a soft gesture of the hand, as if saying, "*He* did it. Isn't it wonderful? Isn't *he* wonderful?" George would frequently take his eyes away from the score and watch me covertly and my reaction to the music, while pretending he wasn't really doing it at all.

It was very late into the night before we finished with the opera. . . . We all felt exultantly happy. The next morning both George and Ira had completely lost their voices. For two days they couldn't talk; they only whispered. I shall never forget that evening—the enthusiasm of the two brothers about the music, their anxiety to do it justice, their joy at its being appreciated and with it all their touching devotion for each other. It is one of those rare tender memories one so cherishes in life.

The opera went into production, and though it was difficult to find singers with fine voices who had enough musical training to perform the complex music, gradually it was cast. Todd Duncan, the Porgy, was a well-trained baritone and a teacher of music who sang a seventeenth-century Italian art song for his audition. The Bess, Anne Brown, heard that Gershwin was looking for a soprano to sing the heroine in his opera and came to him unintroduced. For the sly, menacing Sportin' Life, Gershwin chose a lithe tap dancer named John W. Bubbles, who had had no singing experience at all.

The opera went into rehearsal. It was originally titled *Porgy*, but the producers began to worry whether it would be confused with the play of that name, which had been adapted from the book. So the opera was rechristened *Porgy and Bess*. The change pleased Gershwin. The new name seemed to him to be in the best operatic tradition along with *Tristan und Isolde*, *Samson et Dalila* and *Pelléas et Mélisande*.

Rehearsals continued and new difficulties arose. Most of the cast had cultivated accents, and now they had to learn painstakingly to talk like proper inhabitants of Catfish Row, the broken-down, once-grand mansion which is the main setting for *Porgy and Bess*. Some had never appeared on a stage before, and the director, Rouben Mamoulian, had to show them how to move and use their bodies freely and naturally. John W. Bubbles, the Sportin' Life, on the other hand, had plenty of theatrical experience. His trouble was that he couldn't read music. Time and time again he would miss musical cues and throw off the rest of the cast. Bubbles, a tap dancer, understood music best through his feet, and when he couldn't seem to catch on to the tune of "It Ain't Necessarily So," one of the musical coaches hit on the clever idea of tap dancing the accents of the song until Bubbles grasped how it went.

Gershwin had warned Heyward not to make the opera too long, not to give "the people too much of a good thing." Now, ironically, George discovered that he had fallen into the trap himself, and cuts, which hurt him deeply, had to be made.

Finally all was in readiness, and on September 30, 1935, in the Colonial Theater in Boston, the orchestra struck up the swirling prelude so suggestive of the hurly-burly life in Catfish Row, then softened to the gently chiming accompaniment of Clara's lullaby

> Summertime an' the livin' is easy,
> Fish are jumpin', an the cotton is high.[1]

and the curtain rose for the first time on *Porgy and Bess.*

In a newspaper article published soon after the premiere of his opera, Gershwin set forth very clearly what he had intended to do in *Porgy and Bess.* He had called it a folk opera, and by that he meant that he had based his score on Negro folk music—spirituals, "shouts," working songs, street cries, scat singing—though in fact all the music in the opera was entirely his own invention. He believed that opera should be entertaining, should have humor and contain songs, and he pointed to past examples such as *The Marriage of Figaro* and *Carmen* and *La Bohème*. Finally, because it was a folk opera, he had sought to tell more than just the story of crippled Porgy and his Bess. They are its leading characters, but the

George Gershwin, DuBose Heyward, and Ira Gershwin celebrate the completion of *Porgy and Bess.*
IRA GERSHWIN COLLECTION

true protagonist of the opera was meant to be the Negro himself, in all his moods, his sorrows, his ecstasies.

What the audience heard, therefore, that first night in Boston was something new in the history of American music —a work that was like an opera, but less grand and formal and more comfortable; a work that was in some ways like a musical comedy, but much more serious, tragic even, and not easy to grasp all at once; a work that was a play, but had music; a work that seemed to be a musical love story, but was instead a story of many aspects of life.

To the eternal credit of the city of Boston, the audience and critics were not confused by this strange new kind of folk opera and recognized its greatness. At the final curtain the applause, the cheers and bravos lasted for over fifteen minutes. "Unique . . ." "Striking event . . ." "Easily Gershwin's most important contribution to the theater" were some of the comments. Old friends like S. N. Behrman had come up to Boston to see it. "It's immense," he told George. "It should be played in every country in the world." Serge Koussevitzky, Eva Gauthier, Irving Berlin were equally moved and excited.

A week later, the production headed south to New York. On the way it was decided that the opera was still too long and more cuts were made, including the gravely beautiful song that Porgy addresses to a buzzard, the symbol of unhappiness and death in the first scene of Act Two:

> Buzzard keep on flyin' over,
> Take along yo' shadow.
> Ain' nobody dead dis mornin',
> Livin's jus' begun.
> Two is strong where one is feeble;

Man an' woman livin', workin',
Sharin' grief an' sharin' laughter,
An' love like Augus' sun.[2]

Porgy and Bess opened at the Alvin Theater in New York City on the night of October 10, 1935, and the typically mixed audience that always attended a Gershwin premiere gave it an ovation similar to the one that the opera had received in Boston. The newspapers sent both a drama and a music critic to cover the event from their special points of view, and it is to the eternal discredit of the latter that they failed to recognize what a masterpiece Gershwin had written.

FIRST CRITIC: "It does not utilize all the resources of the operatic composer."

SECOND CRITIC: "The song hits which he has scattered through the score . . . mar it. They are cardinal weaknesses."

THIRD CRITIC: "*Porgy* is falsely conceived and rather clumsily executed."

FOURTH CRITIC: "The score sustains no mood. There is neither a progressive nor an enduring tension to it."

FIFTH CRITIC: "As entertainment it is hybrid, fluctuating constantly between music, drama, musical comedy and operetta."

In the failure of the music critics to recognize its worth, *Porgy and Bess* joined the company of other great operas. After all, there were boos for Verdi's *La Traviata* and Puccini's *Madame Butterfly* at their premieres. How much Gershwin was hurt by the treatment of the critics is not known. Certainly he ought to have become hardened to their attitude

[2] Copyright © 1935 by Gershwin Publishing Corporation. Copyright renewed. Published by Gershwin Publishing Corporation and New Dawn Music Corporation. Used by permission of the publishers.

toward him as a mere Broadway composer. A friend went with Gershwin to a performance of *Porgy and Bess* a few nights after it had opened in New York. They stood in the back of the house, and in the light reflected from the stage she saw tears in his eyes. Was he weeping with pride at the beautiful opera he had written? Or were his tears for the mixed reception it had received and the fact that the theater was not full? She did not know.

Had *Porgy and Bess* been put on at the Metropolitan Opera House it might have received, at the maximum, perhaps eight performances in a season. *Porgy and Bess* was given 124 times on Broadway and toured for three months afterward to various large cities around the country. Nevertheless, *Porgy and Bess* was also a failure commercially, and Gershwin lost not only the work of two years but actual money that he had invested in it.

But George continued to believe in the greatness of his opera. Once the tour was ended and the company disbanded, it seemed headed for extinction. No other opera companies had asked to perform it. Only by a few of its songs might it be remembered. To help keep *Porgy and Bess* alive, Gershwin made a suite out of various numbers from the opera and performed it at concerts which he conducted around the country during the next year and a half.

Today we know only too well how justified Gershwin's faith in his opera was. He had, in fact, produced the first great American opera—and an enduring work of art. His dream was fulfilled.

How the critics of the time could have failed to recognize the greatness of *Porgy and Bess* is hard for us to comprehend now. They judged it by the standards of old-fashioned opera and failed to see that Gershwin had done something new.

Faults the work has. It is a *first* opera. Here and there the orchestration is thick and muddy. Occasional uninspired passages bridge the episodes of the story. But they are minor in comparison to the beauty, the vitality, the sweep of the music, the marvelous choral writing, the charm of the lighter songs, such as "I Got Plenty o' Nuthin' " and "There's a Boat That's Leavin' Soon for New York," and the passion of the love duets "Bess, You is My Woman Now" and "I Loves You Porgy." All of Gershwin's musical studies, combined with his vast theatrical experience, come to fruition in *Porgy and Bess.* He had set out to write an opera that was not just a love story but a characterization of Negro life in a Southern city—and he had succeeded. Just as Italians feel that operas like *La Traviata* and *Madame Butterfly* belong to them, Americans—not just Negroes, but all Americans—have the same feeling about *Porgy and Bess.* It is a part of them and will continue to be throughout the years.

As in the case of its Italian predecessors, *Porgy and Bess* succeeded in a few years after its premiere. But, for the dynamic composer who had believed in his opera more than anyone—that success came too late. George Gershwin never knew of it.

10 / They Can't Take That Away From Me

"THEY ARE AFRAID YOU WILL ONLY DO HIGHBROW SONGS SO WIRE ME ON THIS SCORE SO I CAN REASSURE THEM"

"RUMORS ABOUT HIGHBROW MUSIC RIDICULOUS STOP AM OUT TO WRITE HITS"

During the spring of 1936 the telegrams flew back and forth between New York and Hollywood. Gershwin may have written an opera but he still wanted to keep up the popular side of his career. Broadway was in the doldrums, but a craze for movie musicals had swept America and George wanted to write one. It was precisely because George *had* written an opera, his Hollywood agent explained, that the movie producers were suspicious of him. Opera meant "highbrow" to them and there was no room for anything highbrow in their film productions. George's indignant, cocky reply soon put the matter to rights, and by August contracts had been signed for the Gershwin brothers to write two musicals, both starring their charming dancing friend from Broadway days Fred Astaire.

So once more the Gershwins returned to the slightly unreal land of orange groves and backyard swimming pools and some of the world's most beautiful women sunning themselves around those pools. The days were hot, suntans commonplace; and in the cool evenings there was always a dinner or a late party. Hollywood was in its boom period. The movies were making millions in profits. Stars drew fabulous salaries—so did composers like George Gershwin. Everyone seemed very rich, very glamorous, very much to be envied.

Yet over the whole movie colony, like the now-famous eye-irritating smog of the Los Angeles area, hung a tense, nerve-racking atmosphere. Stars were always on the way up or the way down. There was a tremendous jostling for position. "Everybody's afraid, aren't they? . . . Everybody watches for everybody's blunders, or tries to make sure they're with people that do them credit," F. Scott Fitzgerald has a character say in one of his stories about Hollywood, which he knew well. As for serious actors or writers who came there, they daily had to answer the question which their consciences asked: "What are you doing here—here in a land controlled by people who are afraid of the highbrow, of art, of sincere human expression that aims at something more than just to please?"

To most people George appeared a contented man. He fell in with Hollywood life, played golf, got a suntan, went to parties, took up with not one, but two beautiful movie stars. It was just like the old days in New York—being the center of a glamorous life among famous and attractive people.

He had said that he was "out to write hits" and this is precisely what he proceeded to do. For the two movies *Shall We Dance* and *A Damsel in Distress* he wrote some of his most memorable songs—"Let's Call the Whole Thing Off," "They Can't Take That Away From Me," "A Foggy Day," and "Nice Work If You Can Get It"—which are still favorites today. Backing him up with some of the smoothest lyric writing of his career was Ira, who found the warm sun, nearby beaches and more countrified atmosphere of Hollywood just right for his relaxed tempo of living. ("He hates to go from one room to the next," Leonore Gershwin has been heard to say of her husband.) In fact, Ira found Hollywood so agreeable that he began to make plans to settle there and build a house with a separate studio for George whenever he came to visit.

But if outwardly George seemed as always his brilliant, happy and on-top-of-the-world self, it was a front which masked an increasingly lonely man and a musician frustrated by Hollywood's ways. Movie producers, he was maddened to discover, thought only in terms of "spectacular" and "colossal": if he scored the accompaniment for one of his songs for six violins to keep the texture of the music lighthearted and frothy, they would want to use forty. Surely forty violins must be better than six, went the thinking, as the song was dulled and weighted down by the sheer quantity of instruments. He was amazed to discover when starting work on *Shall We Dance* that only the vaguest kind of over-all story had been worked out for the movie. He and Ira were supposed to furnish songs for places in a plot that hadn't even been decided on. It was worse than writing for the twenties kind of musical comedy—he, who had composed in that most complex of musical forms, grand opera. When a Latin American dance sequence he wrote for the picture was thrown out because one of the bosses had changed his mind the usually good-natured Gershwin stamped off the set and only with difficulty was persuaded to return.

In the meantime he dreamed of writing more serious music. The critics may have considered *Porgy and Bess* a failure, but he believed in it. Also, he had proved to himself that he could write an opera. He planned to compose another with DuBose Heyward based on a story that would take place in the Virgin Islands. The work of a playwright named Lynn Riggs also interested him as a possible source for an opera libretto. Riggs had written an interesting folk play called *Green Grow the Lilacs,* which had been produced on Broadway and which one day would reappear fitted with music—though not by Gershwin—under the name *Oklahoma!* Ever since his teens Gershwin had wanted to write a quartet. Now ideas for one began to come to him. As soon as he could get away from his movie work he planned to rent a small cabin in the mountains and compose in the quiet, undisturbed atmosphere that produced his best music. "It's going through my head all the time," he told a friend about the quartet. "It's about to drive me crazy, it's so damned full of new ideas!"

"Drive me crazy . . ." He had used the words in the exaggerated way that all people do. Soon they would come back to haunt the memory of his friend.

George found his greatest pleasure during this period in appearing as either soloist or conductor in all-Gershwin concerts at various large West Coast cities which he was able to reach by plane. Performing to enthusiastic, sold-out houses, he could at least feel in touch with Gershwin, the serious musician and composer instead of Gershwin, the Hollywood songwriter.

It was his eagerness to show this serious side of himself to Hollywood that made two concerts scheduled by the Los Angeles Philharmonic Orchestra in February, 1937, particularly important to him. At one he was to perform the Concerto in F with Alexander Smallens on the podium. At the other he would appear as conductor.

Hollywood was a part of greater Los Angeles, and as Gershwin had hoped, there was great excitement and interest in the concerts. A Hollywood songwriter playing and conducting the "highbrow" Los Angeles Philharmonic. This was something to wonder at. Weeks in advance the concerts were sold out. The first concert went off smoothly and with the greatest possible success. The next night George appeared, his usual immaculate self in white tie and tails and took his place at the piano to perform the Concerto. Following a quick exchange of glances between conductor and soloist, Smallens gave the cue for the strange and dramatic beginning, with its softly clashed cymbals and thudding kettledrums. Moments later Gershwin made his entrance, tossing off the difficult music with all his usual skill and energy. And then a strange thing happened. In the middle of a relatively simple passage, it seemed to him that the lights in the hall suddenly blacked out and that the electrical system caught fire. At least there was that powerful stink of burning rubber in his nostrils, which often comes from a short circuit. And then, just as quickly, the lights came on again, the smell vanished and George quickly resumed playing. His failure had been momentary and Smallens covered it over so that few in the audience recognized the slip. Afterward he realized that he had suffered a kind of blackout, a loss of consciousness. But how to account for the stench in his nostrils? No one else had smelled it. How could he have imagined anything so unpleasant?

Two months passed. Gershwin's health was perfect, even if he sometimes felt nervous and edgy. That must be the Hollywood atmosphere, he told himself—though he had not been able to resist the lure of easy money and popular success by writing the songs for "one last" movie—the Hollywood atmosphere and the old, gnawing problem that with the passing of each year he still had not made any kind of lasting personal relationship.

To casual observers it seemed very glamorous to be involved with not one, but two beautiful movie actresses. In fact, the one that he was in love with and desperately wanted to marry was the wife of another man. George had always been used to winning the love of any woman he wanted. He believed that the actress would leave her husband and was amazed when she refused. What had happened? Was he no longer attractive to women? The affair with the second actress seemed like a kind of proof to himself that he was.

But his confidence was shaken, and the mirror, which showed him every day that he was losing more and more hair, did not help. To try to prevent his increasing baldness, he bought a powerful suction machine which he used to draw the blood to his scalp every morning. That April, while having what was left of his hair trimmed in a barber shop a violent headache stabbed through his brain. Frantically he looked around at the smiling barbers, the pretty manicurist working away unconcernedly. What was wrong with them? Didn't they smell that disgusting stink of scorched rubber? Gradually he realized that it was entirely in his imagination. Ill and frightened, he left the shop. Could there be some connection between the imagined smell, the headache and the blackout?

As spring came on he continued to work, to play tennis and golf, to take his accustomed place at the piano at parties in the evening. He was working on the third and what he continually vowed would be his last movie, *The Goldwyn Follies,* a kind of musical extravaganza. To one of Gershwin's most warmly beautiful melodies, Ira set words that expressed, ironically, what George now longed desperately to happen in his life.

Love walked right in
And drove the shadows away;
Love walked right in
And brought my sunniest day.

One magic moment,
And my heart seemed to know
That love said 'Hello!'—
Though not a word was spoken.

One look, and I
Forgot the gloom of the past;
One look and I
Had found my future at last.

One look, and I
Had found a world completely new,
When love walked in with you.[1]

But for Gershwin, nothing seemed to drive "the shadows away." For the first time in his life he began to be listless and unable to summon up his usual energy. At parties, friends noticed that he was like someone trying to keep up an old act. Hollywood must be really getting him down, thought some people. George ought to get back to New York. Others thought that he was physically exhausted and should see a doctor. When George finally took their advice he was told that his depressions, his fatigue, his sudden fits of anger were due to nerves—nothing more than nerves. His body, said the doctor, was perfectly fit.

All spring, the worrying, mysterious change continued to overtake Gershwin as a shadow steals over the sun in an eclipse. Was his condition the result of loneliness and the frustration of Hollywood life? Or could there be some physical explanation for it? When in the beginning of June he began to have violent headaches, George decided that his various disorders must be the result of stresses and strains in his inner life, and he consulted a psychoanalyst. To his surprise the analyst sent him to have another physical checkup. Again he repeated his symptoms to the new doctor and also remembered to describe the time that he had imagined he smelled an overpowering odor of burning rubber. Again the diagnosis was nerves. Take a holiday, suggested the doctor.

George followed the advice and went off for a few days to San Diego. When he returned everyone thought he seemed like his old self again. Then on June 20 he was struck by the most excruciating headache he had yet suffered, and when it recurred the doctors decided that he must have tests which could only be carried out in the hospital. What the doctors were looking for was conclusive evidence that George was suffering from a brain tumor, but the somewhat limited tests failed to prove that this was so. Another, more accurate test existed—tapping the fluid in the spine. This George refused to undergo because it would cause terrible headaches and he couldn't stand the idea of more pain. Anyway, he said, the idea of his having a brain tumor was ridiculous.

But was it just "nerves" after all? He returned to the psychoanalyst who saw him daily. Meanwhile the headaches continued, sometimes combined with the disgusting stench in his nostrils. Now, too, he began to lose his coordination. Liquid would slop from a glass when he lifted it to his lips. A knife might suddenly break loose from his hand and fall to his plate with a crash because he had been unable to control it. Bright lights bothered his eyes; he was dazed, apathetic.

Headaches, depression, an imagined nasty odor, loss of coordination, light sensitivity: these symptoms add up to the very clear picture—as any medical student would know—of a brain tumor, an inexplicable growth of cells somewhere beneath the skull. By 1937, thanks to the work of Dr. Harvey Cushing of Boston, techniques for removing brain tumors had been much improved and in some, though not a majority of cases, there was total recovery. The most important factor in cases of brain tumors, once the diagnosis has been made, is time. Each day gained in cutting out the tumor—if it can be removed—offers that much more hope for recovery. What makes brain tumors so difficult to deal with is that X rays cannot penetrate the skull deeply enough to make pictures of any clarity. A doctor has to be very certain of his diagnosis before he goes to the drastic length of opening up the skull.

Because certain tests that Gershwin had been given were negative, it was still hoped that his symptoms might be the result of some kind of nervous disorder. His psychoanalyst decided to isolate him from the tense, busy life going on in the Gershwin house and move him to the smaller, more remote home of a friend. Here Ira and Leonore came to see him for a few minutes every day, but no one else, except the physicians who appeared regularly to examine his eyes and test his reflexes, trying to confirm whether he really was suffering from the deadly tumor or not.

One precious day followed the next. Gershwin's headaches lessened, but he seemed to sink deeper and deeper into a trancelike state. On July 8, while seated at the piano, playing for his analyst, he suddenly lost control and could not go on. Late the following afternoon, having slept most of the day, he got up from bed to go to the bathroom and collapsed in a coma. He was rushed by ambulance to a Los Angeles hospital, where it was found that his reflexes were entirely gone. And now the diagnosis was finally given: brain tumor. The only treatment: surgery, as soon as possible.

Then began a frantic search for a top brain surgeon. By the time a night and a morning had passed, it had been learned that Dr. Cushing was in Europe, but that a former student of his, Dr. Dandy, would be an excellent choice if he could be found. It was a hot weekend in the middle of July, and Dr. Dandy turned out to be cruising in Chesapeake Bay on a yacht without a radio. A desperate call was put through to the White House, and in an attempt to save America's most famous composer from death, two destroyers were sent to locate the yacht and bring Dr. Dandy to land. Calling the Los Angeles hospital from a small Maryland town, Dr. Dandy agreed to take a private plane to Newark, New Jersey, where another private plane would be waiting to fly him across the country—a journey that at that time, meant he would reach the West Coast around noon the next day.

Soon it became clear that noon the next day would be too late. In the meantime, another well-known brain surgeon, Dr. Howard Nafziger, had been located in California and consulted on the case. Examining the unconscious composer, he decided that the necessary surgery must begin at once. Two operations were involved: first, penetrating the skull so that X rays could be made to locate the position of the tumor; then, the removal of the actual growth itself.

At ten-thirty on the evening of July 10, the first operation was begun. Gershwin was taken to the X-ray room so that an hour and a half later, detailed pictures could be made. In the meantime, Dr. Dandy, who had only gotten as far as Newark had been told the latest developments. Instead of flying on, he remained by an open long-distance wire throughout the night, ready to give advice if it was needed.

It was not until 2:30 A.M. that the X rays finally revealed the precise position of the tumor in the right side of Gershwin's brain and three o'clock before all was in readiness for the long, incredibly delicate process of reaching it.

Four hours passed. Down below, in the waiting room of the hospital, sat Ira and Leonore and a group of close friends, frightened and heartsick. This was 1937—the age of modern medicine. Musical geniuses like Schubert and Mozart and Chopin had died at a tragically young age. But not George Gershwin—not in 1937, the age of modern medicine.

Day had long since broken when the doctors appeared and announced that the operation was over. There was nothing to do now, they advised, but go home and wait—and hope. To one close friend, however, the doctors told the truth. When they had finally reached the site of the tumor, they had found that the growth could not be removed. It had grown in a portion of the brain that cannot be touched: the result would have been total disability or death. There had been nothing to do—in 1937, the age of modern medicine.

Ira and Leonore Gershwin left the hospital in separate cars, and the friend had a chance to reveal to Leonore what he had learned from the doctors. Once at home, it seemed more than she could bear to tell Ira; instead, she insisted that she was sure George would recover, that everything would be all right. The telephone rang. It was a call from Max Dreyfus, the kindly music publisher who had subsidized the teen-aged Gershwin. Dreyfus had just heard the news. "What are they doing to my boy?" he demanded.

Half dazed, yet half believing what he was saying, Ira replied that George was going to be all right. The operation had been a success.

A few hours later, the hospital telephoned to say that George was dead. He had never regained consciousness.

One of the most haunting and moving moments in *Porgy and Bess* is Serena's lament for her husband, Robbins, a man struck down quickly and needlessly in the midst of his young life:

> Ole man Sorrow's
> Come to keep me comp'ny,
> Whisperin' beside me
> When I say my prayers . . .[2]

It was as if the wailing, grief-stricken melody sounded softly behind the unbelieving reactions of people as the news went out over the radio: "The man who said he had more tunes in his head than he could put down on paper is dead today in Hollywood . . ."

Gershwin's death affected people everywhere: not only his friends and collaborators like George S. Kaufman—"the greatest tragedy I have ever known"—or Ferde Grofé—"I may never again meet the like of Gershwin"—but men and women who, without knowing him personally, loved him for his music. "I am one of those people," Gershwin once said, "who honestly believe that the majority has much better taste and understanding, not only of music, but of any of the arts, than it is credited with having." From his earliest childhood he had responded to music of the people; in turn, he had tried to reach them with music that they would respond to. How well he had succeeded was obvious enough whenever his music

[2] Copyright © 1935 by Gershwin Publishing Corporation. Copyright renewed. Published by Gershwin Publishing Corporation and New Dawn Music Corporation. Used by permission of the publishers.

was played. Now, with his death, from the messages, the telegrams, the black-rimmed articles in even the smallest newspapers all over the country, the evidence was overwhelmingly clear.

On July 15 a funeral was held at the Temple Emanu-El in New York City, and thousands of mourners crowded Fifth Avenue and 65th Street in the rain, which fell steadily and strangely cold for a summer day. Inside, hundreds of George's friends gathered to hear a beautiful service of prayers, eulogies and selections of music by Bach, Handel and Beethoven —and the theme from Gershwin's own *Rhapsody in Blue.* Later, there were memorial concerts at the Lewisohn Stadium, in the Hollywood Bowl and over the radio.

His best music was still before him! exclaimed dismayed music lovers who had heard *Porgy and Bess* and for the first time recognized what truly extraordinary musical powers Gershwin possessed. But the vast majority of the country had known all along. His best music was already in their hearts, a part of America as long as America existed.

The words of the last song George Gershwin ever wrote sum up what people all over the world feel for his music:

> It's very clear
> Our love is here to stay;
> Not for a year,
> But ever and a day.[3]

11 / Finaletto

"George Gershwin died on July 11, but I don't have to believe it if I don't want to," declared the writer John O'Hara shortly after Gershwin's death. Some twenty years later, Ira, living in Hollywood, received an unexpected telegram from O'Hara saying, "I *still* don't have to believe it if I don't want to."

The fact is hard to believe. Ever since his death, George Gershwin has been appearing in new guises, new transcriptions, new interpretations. His songs turn up constantly in the movies and on television. The charming all-Gershwin musical *An American in Paris* won the Academy Award in 1951. A whole new flock of Gershwin tunes appeared in another movie, *The Shocking Miss Pilgrim.* They were arranged by a close friend of Gershwin from manuscripts and sketches that he left—the first musical ever to be written posthumously.

A steady stream of new recordings of Gershwin's music continues, and as recently as 1958 a Gershwin song was recorded and also published for the first time. This was the early "The Real American Folk Song is a Rag," which can be heard in the wonderful album "Ella Fitzgerald Sings the George and Ira Gershwin Song Books." To listen to these fifty-three songs—including numbers that were written for now-dated twenties musical comedies—is to realize how beautifully Gershwin's music lends itself to fresh arrangements and interpretation.

Joseph James, Helen Colbert, Cab Calloway, and Leslie Scott in a scene from the 1953 production of *Porgy and Bess* at the Ziegfeld Theatre in New York. The show had just returned from a triumphant six-month tour of Europe. BROWN BROTHERS

Finally, there is the miraculous *Porgy and Bess,* George Gershwin's greatest work. Within a year of his death it was revived on the West Coast, and five years later a highly acclaimed presentation on Broadway ran for eight months, then toured twenty-six cities in wartime America. Europe took up *Porgy and Bess* next. The Danish Royal Opera House in Nazi-occupied Copenhagen gave twenty-two performances of the opera to sold-out houses until forced by the Nazis to withdraw it because it was American. Thereafter, the opera became a symbol of the resistance movement. Whenever, the Nazis broadcast news of a victory over the Danish radio, the Danish underground would break in with a recording of "It Ain't Necessarily So."

It's a detail that would have pleased Gershwin.

After the war, opera houses in Sweden, Austria and Switzerland performed *Porgy and Bess,* but not until 1952, when the Department of State sent a brilliant new American production on an international goodwill tour, did the world have a chance to recognize its greatness. London, Berlin, Tel Aviv, Casablanca, Rio de Janeiro, Mexico City—everywhere the company went, audiences cheered the opera, cheered the cast, sang Gershwin's music. *Porgy and Bess* was the first opera by an American composer to be performed at the famous La Scala Opera House in Milan, and it was the first time that any opera was ever performed at the theater nightly for a whole week.

Gershwin would have been pleased by that too.

To wind up its four-year tour, in December, 1955, the *Porgy and Bess* company went to Russia. Some people thought the idea unwise. The story of the opera, after all, was concerned with a group of downtrodden American Negroes living in a segregated slum. Wouldn't this be grist for the

Soviet propaganda mill? On the other hand, there was the joyousness of *Porgy and Bess,* its deep religiousness—above all, its spirit of freedom, which would convey a totally new and more truthful impression of Negro life to the Russians. And there was the cast itself—cultivated, prosperous, scarcely "downtrodden" people—that the Russians could see and meet.

Porgy and Bess was received with the same acclaim in Russia as everywhere else in the world, and the sixty members of the cast, just by being themselves, turned out to be some of the best goodwill ambassadors America has ever had. The author Truman Capote went with the company to Russia and later wrote a witty and fascinating account of the journey and the opening night in Leningrad called *The Muses Are Heard.* In the lobby of the theater, Capote ran into a thoughtful, intelligent, middle-aged Russian whose acquaintance he had made. Capote asked him if he was enjoying *Porgy and Bess.*

" 'I wish I had a ticket for it every night. It's an experience. Powerful! Like Jack London. Like Gogol. I will never forget it,' " the friend said. "A frown creased his forehead," continues Capote, "he opened his mouth to speak, changed his mind, took a swallow of water instead, then changed his mind again, and decided to tell me: 'The question isn't whether I forget. Or what we old ones think. It's the young people who matter. It matters that they have new seeds planted in their hearts. Tonight,' he said, looking round the lobby, 'all these young people will stay awake. Tomorrow, they'll be whistling the music. A nuisance, humming in the classroom. And in the summer, that's what you'll hear: young people whistling along the river. They won't forget.' "

Gershwin would have liked that best of all.

Discography

THIS is not intended as a comprehensive discography of George Gershwin (there are twenty-six recorded versions of the *Rhapsody in Blue* listed in the Schwann March, 1966, catalogue) but as a selection of recordings which I particularly like and which give some idea of the variety of Gershwin's music and of the musical artists who have performed it.

Rhapsody in Blue

Bernstein, Columbia Symphony Orchestra	Columbia ML-5413
	(Stereo) MS-6091
Levant, Ormandy, Philadelphia Orchestra	Columbia CL-700
	(Stereo) CS-8641
Sanroma, Steinberg, Pittsburgh Symphony Orchestra	Everest 6067
	(Stereo) 3067
Wild, Fiedler, Boston Pops Orchestra	Victor LM-2367
	(Stereo) LSC-2367
Bargy, Whiteman Orchestra	Decca 8024
Adler (*harmonica*)	Hamilton 149
	(Stereo) 12149

Oscar Levant was a close friend of Gershwin's and made something of a specialty of playing his music, but the first four recordings listed above are all bright, up-to-date recordings of this tremendously popular piece of music. The Paul Whiteman version gives the listener an idea of how the *Rhapsody* sounded (with a smaller orchestra) when it was first played. I include the Paul Adler harmonica version as an example of one of the many unusual arrangements of the *Rhapsody*.

Concerto in F

Levant, Kostelanetz, New York Philharmonic Orchestra	Columbia CL-700
	(Stereo) CS-8641
List, Hanson, Eastman-Rochester Orchestra	Mercury 50138
	(Stereo) 90002
Wild, Fiedler, Boston Pops Orchestra	Victor LM-2586
	(Stereo) LSC-2586

Excellent, modern recordings of this endearing work.

Three Preludes for Piano

Grant Johannesen	Golden Crest 4065
Leonard Pennario	Victor LM-2731
	(Stereo) LSC-2731
Frank Glazer	Concert Disc-1217
	(Stereo) 217
Jascha Heifetz (*violin*)	Victor LM-2856
	(Stereo) LSC-2856

These engaging pieces can be heard in collections recorded by three fine pianists. The great violinist Jascha Heifetz is an admirer of Gershwin's music and has made transcriptions of the Preludes (as well as some of Gershwin's songs) for his instrument.

An American in Paris

Bernstein, New York Philharmonic Orchestra	Columbia ML-5413
	(Stereo) MS-6091
Dorati, Minneapolis Symphony Orchestra	Mercury 50290
	(Stereo) 90290
Fiedler, Boston Pops Orchestra	Victor LM-2367
	(Stereo) LSC-2367
Whiteman Orchestra	Decca 8024
Toscanini, NBC Symphony Orchestra	Victor LM-9020

All of these with the exception of the Toscanini version have compositions by Gershwin on the reverse side. The Bernstein is particularly ingratiating and the Whiteman again probably the most idiomatic. I list the Toscanini recording because *An American in Paris* is one of the few pieces by an American composer that the great maestro ever recorded. It is not, however, entirely successful; the light, having-a-good-time touch that this music requires seems to have eluded him.

Second Rhapsody for Piano and Orchestra

Bargy, Whiteman Orchestra — Decca 8024
Pennario, Newman, Hollywood Bowl Symphony Orchestra — Capitol P-8581
(Stereo) SP-8581

Cuban Overture

Fiedler, Boston Pops Orchestra — Victor LM-2586
(Stereo) LSC-2586
Hanson, Eastman-Rochester Orchestra — Mercury 50290
(Stereo) 90290
Whiteman Orchestra — Decca 8024

"I Got Rhythm" Variations for Piano and Orchestra

Pennario, Newman, Hollywood Bowl Symphony Orchestra — Capitol P-8581
(Stereo) SP-8581
Wild, Fielder, Boston Pops Orchestra — Victor LM-2586
Stereo LSC-2586

Fine recordings of some of the minor Gershwin compositions.

Porgy and Bess

Engel, Winters, Williams — 3-Columbia OSL-162

Porgy and Bess (excerpts)

Warfield, Price, RCA Victor Orchestra — Victor LM-2679
(Stereo) LSC-2679

Fitzgerald, Armstrong, Orchestra — Verve 4068
(Stereo) 64068

Original Cast — Decca 9024
(Stereo) 79024

Porgy and Bess (symphonic picture)

Dorati, Minneapolis Symphony Orchestra — Mercury 50394
(Stereo) 90394

There is only one recording of the complete *Porgy and Bess,* which is reasonably effective though somewhat dated now in sound. No stereo version of it exists. Leontyne Price was the Bess in the beautiful 1951 revival of the opera and William Warfield the Porgy. These two great artists make the Victor "excerpts" an outstanding recording. Ella Fitzgerald and Louis Armstrong in a jazz version of *Porgy and Bess* show what kind of a different treatment can be given to the music, though it is not what Gershwin intended. On the "original cast" disc you can hear the voiçes of Anne Brown and Todd Duncan, the singers picked by Gershwin, but the recording is naturally rather old in sound. The symphonic picture is made up of excerpts from the opera and is very attractive.

Girl Crazy

Mary Martin and others — Columbia OL-7060
(Stereo) OS-2560

Oh Kay

Columbia OL-7050
(Stereo) OS-2550

An American in Paris (film)

Soundtrack with Gene Kelly — Metro 552
(Stereo) S-552

The Gershwin musicals sound somewhat dated to our ears but the songs never lose their appeal. The delightful film musical *An American in Paris* derived its score completely from Gershwin compositions.

Songs

Gershwin songs appear in recorded collections by such famous singers as Judy Garland, Frank Sinatra, Peggy Lee, Sammy Davis, Jr., and Louis Armstrong, and in arrangements for orchestra by Percy Faith, André Kostelanetz and others. One of the most satisfying of all Gershwin albums is the five-disc set by Ella Fitzgerald, *Gershwin Song Books* (Verve 29-5 [4024/8], Stereo 629-5 [64024/8]). She sings fifty-three Gershwin songs with charm and artistry, giving the listener an idea of the continuing appeal and variety of Gershwin's songs.

Index

Songs, musical compositions, lyrics and books appear under the name of the composer or author. Songs from musicals are listed under the title of the musical.